How does a house become a home?

Christiana Coop and Aimee Lagos of the beloved Hygge & West know that making a home is personal. It's about incorporating the simple things and finding joy and comfort in life's pleasures. It's about recognizing moments that feel cozy, charming, good, and special. It's about designing warm and inviting spaces to reflect that.

In this book, they reveal how different people build a nest of tranquility and comfort, in dwellings big and small, urban and rural, eclectic and minimalist. From bringing elements of the outdoors in to embracing the tiniest spot, creating delightful rooms to spend time together, and incorporating individual touches to add your own unique charm, each place and its story offer inspiration for what it means to bring to life a home that feels deeply meaningful.

With enchanting photography and tips to design special moments in each room, this book is an intimate portrait of what it means to make a personal, beautiful, and inviting home.

HYGGE & WEST

HOME

HYGGE & WEST
HOME

DESIGN FOR A COZY LIFE

Christiana Coop and Aimee Lagos

Photographs by
James Carrière

CHRONICLE BOOKS

SAN FRANCISCO

Library of Congress Cataloging-in-Publication Data
Names: Coop, Christiana, author. | Lagos, Aimee (Aimee Beth), author.
Title: Hygge & west home / Christiana Coop and Aimee Lagos of Hygge & West.
Description: San Francisco : Chronicle Books, 2018.
Identifiers: LCCN 2017051571 | ISBN 9781452164328 (hardcover : alk. paper)
Subjects: LCSH: Interior decoration—Human factors. | Interior
  decoration—Themes, motives.
Classification: LCC NK2113 .C655 2018 | DDC 747—dc23 LC record available
at https://lccn.loc.gov/2017051571

Manufactured in China

Design by Vanessa Dina
Typeset by Howie Severson

10 9 8 7 6 5 4 3 2 1

Chronicle books and gifts are available at special quantity discounts to corpo-
rations, professional associations, literacy programs, and other organizations.
For details and discount information, please contact our corporate/premiums
department at corporatesales@chroniclebooks.com or at 1-800-759-0190.

Chronicle Books LLC
680 Second Street
San Francisco, California 94107
www.chroniclebooks.com

For our parents.

FAMILY

CHARM

INTRODUCTION

The idea for this book was born out of our respect for and connection to the Danish concept of *hygge*, which loosely translates to "cozy" but means so much more. We've often used hygge as a north star for interior design inspiration, since we think that it's important to create spaces that foster an easy reverence for small moments and elevate the every day. Hygge is different for each person, and we love that it's not a formally dictated thing or feeling, rather it invites you to consider what is comforting and meaningful in your own life and how to accommodate and nurture that with your interior design choices.

While hygge is deeply individual, there are some things that are consistently considered essential to achieving it, and we've used those things to organize the homes we've featured on the pages of this book. Enjoying nature, creating cozy spaces, spending time with family, and finding unique ways to experience contentment are all commonly cited as hygge, and we agree. We've featured people who truly embrace living in and appreciating the moment and showcased all the different ways in which their homes embody this commitment to living with purpose. We hope that we've demonstrated that creating a warm, welcoming, personal space is something everyone can do. We also hope that you enjoy reading this book as much as we enjoyed creating it. We are deeply grateful to everyone who let us spend time in their home, and we will always treasure this as one of our most wonderful—and wonderfully hygge—experiences.

THE HYGGE
&
WEST STORY

We grew up together in Los Alamos, New Mexico—a small town in the mountains north of Santa Fe. We first met in preschool, but didn't become close friends until second grade, when we bonded over our mutual love of ballet. We both still remember our first official playdate—we created an elaborate Smurf village in the sandbox of Christiana's backyard.

Our entrepreneurial instincts first became evident in the very early years of our friendship. We had dreamed up an imaginary boutique we'd own together one day called the Denver, because Denver was the biggest city either of us had ever visited at that age. Sadly, it was also not an especially original name, as there actually was a department store called the Denver at the time. Nonetheless, we'd spend hours drawing full catalogs of clothing and accessories with detailed descriptions. One of our biggest regrets is that neither of us know what happened to that catalog; we sure would love to flip through its pages today.

We were joined at the hip for the better part of elementary, middle, and high school. We spent our summers together at the neighborhood pool or riding bikes around our scenic hometown.

We double-dated at almost every high school dance we attended, and when we weren't invited to a dance, we spent the evening commiserating together, watching movies, and highlighting our hair. Always like-minded, we both became deeply obsessed with *Top Gun*, and continue to speak in *Top Gun* quotes (much to the chagrin of those closest to us). There are few memories from our collective adolescence that do not include the other.

Following high school, we went our separate ways, with Aimee heading off to North Carolina and Christiana to Colorado. Aimee went straight to law school after college, while Christiana was able to finagle a much cooler life, living in Aspen, Colorado, for two years before she eventually also attended law school. We ended up at the same huge law firm in Chicago, though our overlap was short. Aimee had quickly determined that being a big firm litigation associate was not the right fit for her, and left to start a family. Christiana eventually transferred from Chicago to the San Francisco branch of her firm and settled in the Bay Area, and Aimee moved to Minneapolis with her young family and started a new career in marketing.

After a while, we were both looking for some change in our lives, which, for both of us, ended up being precipitated by a change in decor. Aimee was searching for new bedroom furniture, and as always, it was a mutual project as we constantly emailed ideas back and forth, discussing the pros and cons of different potential interior schemes. During this hunt, Aimee came across a Danish wallpaper company, ferm LIVING, and both of us fell in love with their unique designs. When we tried to place an order, we discovered that they did not have a U.S. distributor, and so a plan was hatched. The next time we were together, we built a detailed marketing and distribution plan (perhaps exaggerating our expertise in both areas) and then reached out to ferm LIVING. To our surprise and delight, they agreed to our plan, and in the spring of 2007, we became their first U.S. distributor.

We'd been working with ferm LIVING for a little over a year when the economy started to sputter, and it became increasingly difficult to run the distributorship profitably. We'd also realized that the work wasn't as creative as we'd initially hoped it would be—we were essentially salespeople, and the majority of our time was spent dealing with overseas shipping companies and figuring out how long shipments would be stuck in customs. We started to discuss what our next step might look like. Our time with ferm LIVING had taught us so much and had also given us solid connections within the interior design industry. We'd fallen in love with wallpaper during this time, and we saw an unexplored niche in the industry. Wallpaper was just starting to see a resurgence as a design trend. As a product, it was neither very accessible nor affordable. We thought that we could offer a high-quality, well-designed, and reasonably priced product direct to the consumer, and the idea of starting our own wallpaper company was born.

We discovered artist and illustrator Julia Rothman around this same time, when Christiana had used one of her patterns, a charming bird flying among the clouds, to test a custom wallpaper service that ferm LIVING had been trying to launch. We fell in love with it and chose it as our first pattern. We decided that our model would be to partner with designers and artists whose work we loved to develop collections of wallpaper. We met with Julia and asked her to create additional designs for us, and she graciously agreed. At the same time, we started searching for a wallpaper printer and began building our brand.

Our close connection to Danish design started with ferm LIVING, and through it, we came across a simple but powerful word—*hygge*. It perfectly captured what we were trying to emulate in our own lives, and we both became obsessed with it. The notion of appreciating small moments, recognizing the specialness of everyday activities, and creating a warm and welcoming space for yourself, family, and friends to enjoy resonated with changes we had recently made in our own lives. We just couldn't get it out of our heads, and even though we knew that we'd have to pronounce, spell, and explain it countless times over the lifespan of our business, we decided that it needed to be part of our company name. We added "& West" because our goal was—and still is—to bring an Americanized twist to the concept of hygge.

Hygge & West officially launched in the fall of 2008. We got a bit carried away and had created a host of products in addition to wallpaper, including candles, a set of dessert plates, and T-shirts. We also curated a small assortment of products, mostly from Denmark and England, that we felt embodied the notion of hygge. We received great press at launch and were excited and optimistic about the potential of our little business. And then a couple of months later, the economy crashed. We saw the momentum we'd built completely dissipate and the orders that had been steadily trickling in suddenly screech to a painful halt.

It would be untrue to say that the next few years weren't very difficult. We both had quit our jobs and had to find new ones in an incredibly challenging job market to support ourselves while the business floundered. There were plenty of nervous conversations, more credit card debt than either of us were comfortable with, and difficult decisions about what to do to get the business going again. As hard as it was, we learned a great deal. Most importantly, we learned that it was better to focus on one thing and really own it. Returning to the product that had initially inspired us, we decided that wallpaper would be our one thing, and thankfully we were able to stay afloat long enough for the economy to turn around once more.

Over the years, our model of working on collections with designers and artists we love has served us well, and we've had the great fortune to collaborate with an amazing group of people. We are honored to have built a vibrant little creative community that includes fine artists, social media influencers, some of our favorite small companies and boutiques, illustrators, and graphic designers. With what we've learned over the years, we also began creating our own patterns, and now have a robust collection of Hygge & West–designed items. We are incredibly lucky to be doing work we love, with people we love, and can't imagine doing anything else professionally.

We've also been incredibly lucky to have an active community of customers and supporters of the company. It is always the highlight of our day to see images of how people use our products in their own homes on social media or in our email inboxes. And we love it when we receive positive feedback from wallpaper installers praising our product or from homeowners letting us know how happy it makes them. Seeing our wallpaper out in the wild is also a favorite, particularly of Christiana's—she has dragged Aimee, family, and friends to any and all public places featuring our wallpaper for impromptu photo shoots (including a particularly awkward selfie of us she insisted on taking in Bergdorf Goodman).

Hygge & West continues to grow and evolve. After initially determining that it was best for us to focus on a single product, we finally grew in size and confidence to the point that we were ready to explore bringing our signature love of pattern to new parts of the home. We dove into learning about different product categories and production methods, and after a lot of work, we launched shower curtains, and then bedding. As far as what the future holds for our little company, we never say "never." We continue to have interesting opportunities arise all the time, and whatever we ultimately choose to pursue, we'll do it together and enjoy every step of the process.

NATURE

Nature is an endless source of inspiration, strengthening one's sense of place and belonging in a vast world. These homes all share a deep connection to nature, not only in their setting and interior design but also in the lifestyles of the families who inhabit them.

AIMEE LAGOS

Entrepreneur | Mother | Co-Owner of Hygge & West

NORTH SAND LAKE, WISCONSIN

Christiana: Ever since I've know her, Aimee has always been a trendsetter. She introduced me to coordinated Esprit outfits in third grade. Middle school was all about matching accessories, a subject in which Aimee excelled. In high school, she led the charge with platform shoes, and by law school, she was rocking the chicest pixie cut. Her strong sense of style stems from her strong sense of self, I think. Growing up, she was one of the strongest people I knew. Combine that with also being the smartest, funniest, and most steadfast, and that's a best friend you're going to keep forever. And those qualities in a business partner? I couldn't be luckier.

When Aimee told me she'd bought a family lake cabin with her husband, Manny, I had no idea what I was in for. My first visit was in the winter. With no TV, a barely working Internet, and frigid temperatures, I was a little hesitant. But the cabin was wonderfully cozy, and the way time slowed down there was a true luxury. We sat around reading magazines, ventured out for sledding and to watch her boys, MJ and Jackson, play hockey on the lake, and drank wine around the fire at night. My next visit was in the summer and, well, it was even better. We'd meant to do a little work, but the pull of drinking cocktails in floaties under a shining sun while watching her dogs play proved too tempting to resist. Aimee has created a beautiful retreat befitting its beautiful location. It's a magical place, and I feel so fortunate to be included in not only her family's carefree cabin living, but also her close-knit family.

You grew up in New Mexico, live in Minnesota, and have a lake home in Wisconsin. What are the similarities and differences between life in these places?

Growing up in New Mexico gave me an appreciation of the outdoors, which is something that I really wanted to pass on to our boys. They don't have the same opportunities to just wander around in nature like I did when I was young because they're growing up in a city, so we're really lucky to be able to give them that with our cabin. Having a cabin is a very Minnesotan thing to do. Our cabin neighbors are all Minnesotans, so it doesn't necessarily feel like there's a separation between Minnesota and that part of Wisconsin. I tease my husband, who grew up in Saint Paul, that I'm becoming much more Minnesotan than he is because I've wholeheartedly embraced this aspect of Minnesota culture.

How would you describe your personal style and aesthetic?

Chaos chic? Durable-hemian? Maybe I should just go with eclectic. I don't necessarily subscribe to a specific style or aesthetic—I look for things that I connect with in some way. I'm really intentional about what I bring into our home because I tend to get attached to things and keep them forever. And, of course, with two teenage boys, three dogs, and a cat, I also need things that are going to stand up to plenty of wear and tear. I learned long ago that I could either obsess about keeping things clean and making sure nothing ever got broken, or I could lower my expectations a bit and be a whole lot happier. It's important to me that I feel that our home reflects our style and personality, but life is just way too short to be overly precious about things.

What was it like to design and decorate your cabin?

First and foremost, we wanted the cabin to be a happy, comfortable place where we could relax and connect with family and friends. I intentionally set a smaller budget to see what we could do with less, so I've been designing in phases. The cabin still isn't completely done, but it's at a point where I can look at it and feel content, rather than just seeing all the things that I want to change. When you have a weekend/vacation home, you don't want to be doing home improvement projects all the time—you want to enjoy yourself. As a result, things took longer than usual, and I had to be patient, which isn't one of my strong suits.

I think our biggest success was finding the right place. We looked at probably ten cabins, and this was the first one we saw. We just knew it was the right one and none of the others compared. We have enough room to have a bunch of people come stay with us, but the space is divided up well and the cabin doesn't feel too big. We love the way it sits above the lake so we have a beautiful view, and the lake itself is really clean and clear. Plus, we're only a two-hour drive from home, so if we want to come up for just a night, we can.

How did your two children influence the cabin's design?

We wanted the cabin to be somewhere that the boys could bring a bunch of friends and have a great time. Our kids were a bit older when we got the cabin, so we were really designing for their teen and college years. Having boys means that no one really cares

about what anything looks like or appreciates design choices, but I hope they like the space I created for them and that they enjoy sharing it with friends. We're also lucky that the downstairs has a separate family room, so they can congregate down there and have some distance from the adults. Now that they are teenagers, we find that they need a little more space. We have a heated workshop in the back of the garage, and I think that our next project will be turning that into a Ping-Pong room for them.

What do you think pattern—and wallpaper in particular—brings to a home that other design elements can't?

At Hygge & West, we have always tried to create wallpaper that felt like art, but on a larger scale. So our patterns tend to add a noticeable layer to a room. I love interesting spaces where there is juxtaposition or tension between elements. Wallpaper creates a strong base for building such a space in a way that paint and color alone can't. And even though wallpaper is much more common in homes than it used to be, it still feels different and special—people always notice it and comment on it. I've found that people who use wallpaper tend to take other interesting risks in their interior design choices, so you rarely see a boring room when wallpaper is part of the equation.

How does your decorating style differ between the cabin and the city? Does either place influence the other?

Our home in Minneapolis is a 1908 foursquare, so the contemporary lines of the cabin allowed us to have a more modern decor scheme than we do at home. I like that the cabin is much cleaner and minimal; it's a nice contrast to have two homes with such different personalities. At home, we constantly struggle with having too much stuff, so we've been very intentional in keeping the cabin as free of clutter as possible. At home, we have a tiny backyard, and the dogs destroyed the grass long ago, so we put in a patio and pea gravel. At the cabin, the woods and the lake are our yard, and we spend a lot of time out on the deck or around a fire in the evenings. In many ways, the cabin feels like the counterbalance to the house, or the response to it.

Your cat and dogs must love life at the lake. How does living with pets differ at your cabin versus your home in the city?

The dogs love it—especially our lab, who is a total water baby. It's nice for city dogs to have some space to roam around and be free, and they take full advantage of it. Our friends who join us at the cabin most frequently also have dogs, so it's usually a big dog party up there with up to five dogs roaming around at any given time. The cat likes it a bit less because of the aforementioned dog party and due to the fact that he's an indoor cat, but he enjoys that we seem to curl up on the sofa with him much more often up at the cabin than at home. He's a very good napper.

How do you spend your time in the cabin? What do you do for fun and relaxation?

It depends on the season. In the summer, we are in the water as much as possible—either on the boat, on the dock, or floating around on an inflatable raft. The lake we live on is unbelievably clear, and the water is just right for swimming. We grill, eat outside, play washers, and kick a soccer ball around. In the winter, we hunker down a bit more. I read, while the boys go out on the frozen lake and skate or ice fish. I take a lot of naps and cook long, complicated recipes. We all pile on the sofa beneath cozy blankets and watch movies. The one thing that we always do for fun, no matter the season, is play cards. Some of our dear friends introduced us to a game they call Idiot, and we play at least two or three rounds of it together almost every night. I make breakfast burritos in the mornings as a nod to my New Mexican roots. We sit around the table and enjoy our meals and talk, as opposed to at home where we're usually going in four different directions while shoving food down our throats because someone is late for something. I love it. I wish our day-to-day life was more like our life up north.

CREATING A SIGNATURE DRINK

"My husband and I both spent time in Spain when we were young, and there is a drink there called a kalimotxo. It's basically red wine and Coke over ice. We were looking for a good drink to indulge in up at the cabin and, remembering those days in Spain, we created our own version using inexpensive red wine with Vanilla Coke Zero. Turns out, it's delicious! We call it cabin sangria, and it's become a summertime cabin tradition."

"Escaping to the cabin allows us to live at a much slower pace for a couple of days so we can recharge and reconnect."

STEPHANIE HOUSLEY

Artist | Entrepreneur | Owner of Coral & Tusk

BONDURANT, WYOMING

We met Stephanie Housley in an especially fortuitous way that also proved how small the world often is. While in Paris in the fall of 2015, we visited Maison Bastille—a delightful café in the Marais that features our Rosa wallpaper by Rifle Paper Co. As we enjoyed our delicious breakfast, we noticed an impossibly chic and heartwarmingly happy French family at a nearby table. Halfway through the meal, a striking, smiling woman joined them, carrying a Coral & Tusk doll for the family's little girl. We wondered if this woman could indeed be the owner of Coral & Tusk, but quickly moved on to planning the day's adventures. After we finished eating, we posted images from the café on Instagram, and then headed out to soak up Paris. Hours later, we noticed that Stephanie had commented on our photo, "Were you guys there today?" Turns out, she had been the smiling woman bearing the gift.

Stephanie imbues Coral & Tusk with a playful spirit and a healthy dose of personality to create a whimsical design sensibility that is uniquely her own. She is also a whip-smart and incredibly driven businesswoman who has built a highly successful and widely respected company.

When Stephanie told us that she and her husband, Chris Lacinak, were moving to a log cabin outside of Jackson Hole, Wyoming, we asked her if she'd let us come visit and include her new home in our book. We spent two days with her in that achingly beautiful setting. It snowed while we were there, so we were able to experience a magical, snowy sunset while sharing a delicious meal that Stephanie had prepared for us. Our time in that cozy, lovely place was far too short. We consider ourselves lucky to call Stephanie a friend.

How would you describe your style at home?

Minimal and clean. I am not into clutter, or mess, or stacks of things. I like having very few things and having those things mean something—objects that have a history or story, or exude some feeling of being intentionally made. I like palettes of either crisp whites with salvaged woods or deep teal blue with copper and brass accents. I allow myself to live vicariously through magazines. In the same way that some people get lost in a movie, a good shelter magazine is a total and complete escape for me.

How does your home influence the way you live in it?

We are still very much discovering that. We searched for a place out here for a year. We looked at about seventy-five properties, ranging from just land to a variety of houses in different areas. When we finally found this thirty-year-old log cabin on twenty acres with incredible views, we knew our search was over and this was home. Even though we own our apartment in New York, co-op apartment living is very different from being a real house homeowner. I am learning how to use each space and exist in it, organize it, and, little by little, embellish and add to it with our own belongings and decor. There was so much love and care put into this house and property by the previous owners, who built it, that it has been a gradual process of absorbing what was so intentionally created and gently evolving it into our own.

Coral & Tusk is about handicraft, pattern, and lots of warm texture. How are those elements expressed in your home?

The house itself is a pretty stunning example of all those things: it is a handmade log cabin, and even the chinking (the material used at the joints of two logs) is hand-scribed, hand-cut wood, which is very rare since it is a more antiquated and laborious method. The texture, pattern, and warmth of the logs create a dominant feeling on their own. We've layered in our warm Coral & Tusk fabrics through upholstery or bedding in most rooms of the house. We have heavy Moroccan wool rugs, which really add to those categories as well.

Where do you find inspiration for your home and your business?

My inspiration comes from everywhere, but mostly animals, travel, nature, and feelings. My love of and fascination with animals is abundant and obvious in almost every design I make. From collection to collection, there are several recurring themes within the animal imagery that I use. I am ceaselessly happy to ponder what any given animal might wear, where they might live, how they might decorate this imaginary habitat, who their friends and family are—on and on and on. Spending time watching any wildlife do anything is a source of much enjoyment. Wildlife observation is always a top priority, from watching a squirrel from my Brooklyn apartment to now, in Wyoming, viewing families of deer in my own backyard, foxes crossing the road, and moose sauntering down the street. I love it anywhere and everywhere.

What is it about your house that makes it feel like home?

It's just a feeling, really. There is not much that defines that. I grew up in Ohio and my mom moved out of the state when my dad passed away a few years ago, so I lost my roots and attachment to a home on a base level. Even though we'd lived in New York for almost twenty years and loved it, that, too, started to change and I realized that it did not feel like home, like in-your-guts home. My husband and I had visited Wyoming several times since our childhoods and one day I got a vision of being here. We were sitting on the couch in Brooklyn and I said, "I think we should," and he finished with, "move to Wyoming." Who knows how we were both in this same mindset, but hallelujah, we were, and our search for our home began. And there is no way to define what made this place the one, but it certainly is!

Hygge is all about finding joy and comfort in life's simplest pleasures. How do you find or create hygge in your home?

One aspect I am so excited about in this house is the open floor plan and being able to interact between the kitchen, dining room, and living room, so meal preparation and entertaining can happen at the same time. And we added a fireplace for maximum hygge!

Other than that, a main goal with this house was to have super cozy, comfy, warm beds. With so many guests this summer, we really wanted to do as much as possible to provide a comfortable experience and think ahead about what makes a guest's time here fun to the max, especially being so far from everything. If someone forgot something, we better hope we have it.

You're lucky enough to have a separate studio space on your property. How have you made that space work for your needs?

I am blessed with incredible self-discipline, so working from home has never felt challenging. I will say though, since I've been here I have developed a deep appreciation for a separate studio space. And I am big on inspiration boards. Now that I have all this studio space, I can allocate dedicated places for a variety of activities and projects, which allows me to move from thing to thing without the hassle of reorganizing all the time. The studio has all the fun stuff—my library, fabrics, collections, and pieces of inspiration—and is decorated with these elements while keeping maximum functionality at the forefront. I got an amazing twelve-foot-long antique farm table from Round Top Antiques Fair in Texas and it is the anchor of the space. We installed Homasote along one entire thirty-foot wall, floor to ceiling, so I have plenty of space for inspiration boards, prototypes, and drawings.

Are there any traditions you've created or maintained in this home?

The previous owners filled this home with so much love, and that comes through strongly in the overall feeling of this house and land. It is our goal to honor their hard work and carry on the traditions of being good to each other, good to this place, and good neighbors in this community of very few people.

EMBRACING FAMILY HEIRLOOMS

Stephanie's late grandmother collected
and treasured willow-pattern china, which
was later passed down to Stephanie. Rather
than storing or displaying the collection,
Stephanie uses the china as her regular
dinnerware—a decision that encourages frequent and fond remembrance of her grandmother in life's simple, everyday moments.

Beloved heirlooms can also make for a
unique conversation starter, like this striking
art piece made from an original sack from
the flour mill Stephanie's husband's family
owned for generations. The piece lives in the
couple's guest room, offering visitors
a fun, casual way to get to know their
hosts a bit better.

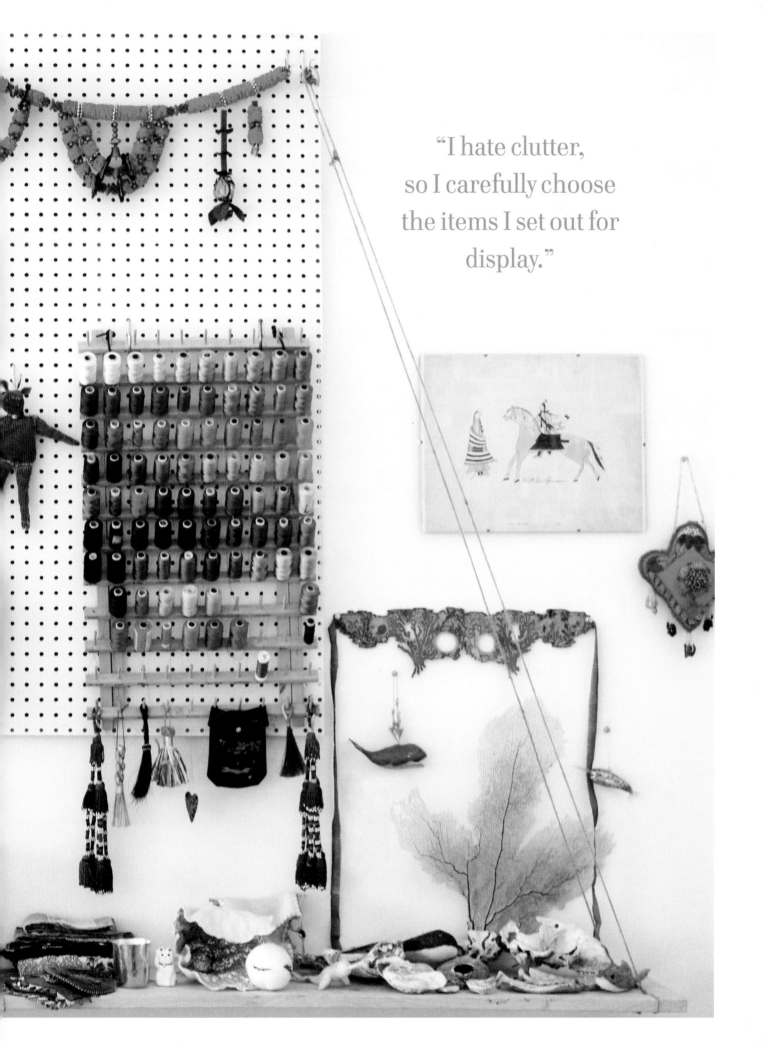

"I hate clutter, so I carefully choose the items I set out for display."

ALEX BEAUCHAMP

Strategist | Maker | Traveler

TOPANGA, CALIFORNIA

We stumbled upon Alex Beauchamp and her blog, *Hygge House*, over a decade ago when we were naming our company and figuring out how to accurately translate the Danish word *hygge* into English. To this day, we still think Alex sums it up best: "Hygge is a Danish word used when acknowledging a feeling or moment, whether alone or with friends, at home or out, ordinary or extraordinary, as cozy, charming, or special."

Since we first became aware of Alex and our hygge connection, we recognized in her a kindred spirit in the pursuit of living and designing with meaning and integrity. She's made a career of consulting with and creating award-winning content for some of the most well-known companies in retail and hospitality, and has brought her ability to make the ordinary extraordinary to countless projects. Her blog is an incredibly charming blend of observations and advice, and it showcases her knack for finding the hygge in all aspects of life. To us, she is a hygge mentor, and we greatly admire her consistent passion for keeping the term true to its Scandinavian roots.

Tell us about your home, the Hygge House. What was your vision for your home and how did you bring it to life?

My home is a hand-built 1920s hunting lodge in the Santa Monica Mountains. The very first time I saw it at an open house, I immediately knew it was meant to be my home. It had a very South-of-France feel, but also this very American-lodge quality. I feel like the outside is Provence, the inside and downstairs are American lodge, and the upstairs is Scandinavia, so it represents all my cultures coming together in one place.

My vision for the home was to keep it as simple and true to itself as possible, to try not to change it into a home that didn't fit the landscape or the history, and to keep all its details on full display instead of my things. The home was well maintained, but not loved, and I wanted to bring it back to its simplistic glory. I spent a lot of time pruning the garden, making living rooms outside and inside, and finding furniture that would blend in with the home, rather than take away. One of the biggest ways I did this was to not use curtains. I've used dramatic drapes in all of my previous homes, but this home felt like it needed to be open and the windows needed to be frames for the art outside them. Everything's organized so I can spend more time living instead searching for things, but it's still a casual, relaxed home.

Your home and your blog are all about the essence of hygge—finding pleasure in simple things. How does your home allow you to do that more easily than living somewhere else might?

It's not my home that allows me to find pleasure in the simple things—it's my state of mind. My home naturally lends itself to the concept of hygge, but I've had city flats that have also been the essence of hygge. I think my current home makes it easier because it's an old, rustic home that seems removed from modern life. You don't see neighbors; you see trees. You don't hear traffic; you hear coyotes. Modern conveniences like the washing machine are hidden, so you see things like stone walls before electric appliances. Instead of running down to the café for coffee, you need to make some in a carafe, which takes time. The home forces a slower-paced life, but it still takes one mentally accepting this and recognizing some of the differences as pleasures instead of challenges.

What makes the Hygge House feel like home?

At the time that my home was built, there weren't modern luxuries like paved roads or power tools, so the owner used a lot of the nature around him to build his home. The first floor has stone walls that make up the foundation and wall structure. All of the stones are from the area and were individually hand set. In the living room, a large boulder is part of the foundation and wall because in 1920 there wouldn't have been a way to remove it.

From low ceilings with exposed beams to gorgeous stonework, your home wears its history with pride.

Maybe it's the *Downton Abbey*–lover in me, but I believe that people are the keepers of great homes; it's not necessarily that this is my home, but rather that I'm in charge of looking after it while I'm here. I'll add my history to it, but I didn't want to take away from the history it already has. Keeping the beams exposed and the furniture away from the boulders in the floor so that you can see those details was really important. The stonework and boulders are my favorite part of the house because they're from the land, they're handmade, and they're part of the home's history and future. That kind of integration with nature is something that helps literally ground me every day.

I love white walls and a minimal aesthetic, so I initially thought that it would be challenging to live with so much dark stone and wood. All my furniture and decor had always been geared toward a home with white walls, but somehow, it all ended up working together and I fell for its natural elements. Cozy is cozy no matter what the decor, and I'll always be a sucker for that.

You've lived all over the world, including in New Zealand, France, Canada, the United Kingdom, and Singapore, before settling in California. Do each of these cultures have their own embodiments of hygge? How have they influenced your lifestyle and home?

Hygge might be a Danish word, but it's really a state of mind that can be found in any culture. And although I find lots of hygge moments when living in different cultures, I'm more inclined to be part of the existing culture than bring something to it. In France, it's all about joie de vivre, and in the United Kingdom, it's about teatime in the afternoon or walks in the countryside. Having lived in all these different countries, I do get influenced. For example, after spending a lot of time in Asia, I became very interested in feng shui, and now I actively practice it in my home. If you look closely, you'll see certain colors, materials, and objects carefully put into different areas of the bagua (the energy map of your space, according to feng shui principles). They don't look like traditional feng shui cures, and my home definitely feels more Danish and French than Asian, but I love how feng shui thinks about energy and space, and I feel as though that concept perfectly complements hygge.

Your entryway features our Otomi wallpaper in red. What do pops of pattern and color like this bring to a home?

I've always had a weakness for wallpaper, especially the elaborate prints and designs found in old estates and manor homes. I love the story that wallpaper can tell, but I've often found it challenging to find the right space and wallpaper combination. When I moved into my home, I had this stunning two-story wall off my staircase, and I knew it'd be perfect for print. My challenge was that the view outside was pure nature—greenery and stone—and the inside was white. So I wanted something to highlight the drama of the space but not compete with nature.

The red Otomi pattern was perfect for so many reasons. The red was vibrant but not harsh; it was a very Danish red. The pattern looked Scandinavian but actually was inspired by mixing folk art with the traditional pattern from the Otomi people in Mexico. Since half of my fella's family comes from Mexico, I thought it'd be a lovely blend of our two cultures—the Danish red and the Mexican print. I love that they tell a story on their own and tell another story on my wall.

Are there any traditions you maintain in this home?

My mother always lit a simple white candle every morning while having coffee. It started as just a Danish habit, but as family began to pass, she started lighting it in their honor. I've now taken on this tradition of lighting a simple candle on my kitchen table first thing every morning, and thinking about family and friends before I start my day. It's a sort of meditation even though it lasts less than twenty seconds.

What are your must-haves for creating coziness on a rainy day?

The tried-and-true things like Earl Grey tea, a warm wool blanket, a dog on my lap, and quiet are what make rainy days so perfect. One of the reasons I bought a butterfly chair and stool was so that I could position them by my huge living room window, so that when it rained, I could just sit and listen. I grew up with the pretty consistent sound of rain, and I find it a great comfort and relaxant. Living in Southern California, rain has eluded me for many years, but I still designed a home around the possibility of hearing it and being part of it. I think making the most out of a gloomy day is really how the idea of hygge came to be.

"There's a huge misconception that hygge is just about home or that it can be bought. I've seen lists of hygge foods or top hygge products for your living room, and that's the opposite of what hygge is about. Hygge is really the act of being present enough in your daily life to recognize moments that feel cozy, charming, good, sweet, and special. And that's what's so important to remember—that creating hygge is just recognizing it."

PATRICK LONG

Illustrator | Maker | Collaborator

OCEANSIDE, OREGON

Aimee: While working on a campaign with Storm Tharp (featured on page 220) back in my retail marketing days, I noticed that he had a particularly amazing work bag. I complimented him on it, and he told me that it was made by Chester Wallace, a company run by his close friend, Patrick Long. The next time I saw Storm, he had a Chester Wallace bag for me—a wonderful surprise! I love its sturdy durability, as well as its straightforward design. We were finalizing shoots in Portland and found that we needed one more person in the area to feature in the book when I remembered my bag. We reached out to Patrick to gauge his interest, and he let us know that he and his partner had just completed a home in Oceanside, right outside Portland. We instantly knew that we had to include his them.

Patrick is a highly regarded illustrator and is a friend of, or has collaborated with, nearly every one of the most respected members of Portland's creative community. His talent is only matched by his graciousness. During our shoot with Patrick and his partner, Jon Hart, on the stunning Oregon coast, we were treated like friends, not strangers. Jon took us on a tour of the beach over lunch, which included a trek through a tunnel to a second, hidden beach. We loved spending the day with them and learning about their lives, the building of this little gem of a home, and their connection to this very special, breathtakingly beautiful place.

Where did your love for design begin?

I am the son of an architect. My father taught me to look at doorknobs and ceilings and the spaces in between. The things one touches every day can add up significantly. A handle or the rise of a step can be a pleasure, and a benefit. Once you start looking, it's easy to expand on the idea. And my father also taught me that it's fun to make things.

Your home is situated on one of the most stunning pieces of land we've ever seen. How did you create interiors that complemented, rather than competed with, those views?

The ocean view is the best part, and it's the biggest part. It is a mesmerizing time waster. The house is very easy to live in—it's not that big, and there is always something to see out the windows, be it from the sink, stove, or couch.

I don't think we set out to decorate, but rather we are collectors of things with stories and history. This house is filled with memories of travels and artwork from friends. When I turn on a small wooden light, I think of the antique store in Stockholm where we bought it. A print of sea lions reminds me of a trip to Budapest, and a walk on our way to the Gellért Baths. When there is a need for something in the house, Jon will often make it. He made the dining room tabletop to fit on antique upholstery jacks that had been sitting around waiting to be put to use.

The exterior of your home is dark and minimalist, almost receding into the natural scenery around it. What inspired its design?

Everything about this house was a conscious decision, rather than arbitrary. Our architect is extremely good at clean and smart observation. The lot is triangular, which led the design. We wanted a building with minimal upkeep, so that informed the materials we used. The salt wind takes its toll, so we did our best to choose what survives best in this environment. Black was an easy choice. People understand it—it's definitive, like a period. Cut into the black are comforting recesses of cedar shake, warm and natural moments that relate back to the trees.

On the other hand, the interior of your home is light, bright, and airy, with a few strategic accents of earthy color—a beautiful contrast with Portland's rainy, overcast weather.

The white was an easy choice to go with all the windows. Shadows look great on it. The big counter is a pale gray, so it's not too stark against the white. We're too messy for stark. Hell, it's a beach house. There is room for a red blanket, and an Icelandic fur.

The windows and the size of the house lend it its lightness. More often than not, we just stay on the upper floor. The space is small, but open. Because of the lot, the house telescopes back with intersecting angles. The ceiling rises in the living area, then falls in the sleeping area. It's a comforting shelter with an expansive view.

TREASURE HUNTING

One of Patrick and Jon's favorite pastimes is
collecting agates from the beach down the hill
from their home. This simple act adds a sense
of purpose and discovery to an otherwise
leisurely stroll and brings the raw, natural
beauty of the ocean indoors.

How does what's outside your window—the lush greenery, the water, the weather—affect the way you design inside?

We do our best to have less. It's not easy. Stuff can be wonderful, but it can distract and become noisy, too. The ocean will always be larger and command our attention.

What is your favorite room in your home?

The main bedroom is a favorite. The house is built on a bit of a slope—the front, ocean-facing side is elevated and wide, while the back of the house narrows and anchors into the hill. All the angles of the triangular shape come together like facets in that bedroom, while one square window looks directly into the neighboring forest.

Much like your bags, your home has a utilitarian sense to it. How do you decide what to bring into your space and what to leave out?

It's not easy, and we're not brilliant at it. Jon is better at saying no. I like souvenirs, especially when they're small and have a purpose. Even a spoon can be loaded with memories. Beauty is in the eye of the beholder—make sure you want it.

ISABELLE DAHLIN

Interior Designer | Traveler | Owner of deKor

OJAI, CALIFORNIA

Born and raised in Sweden, and once a resident of Paris, Isabelle Dahlin eventually settled in Los Angeles after falling in love with the city's diversity and laid-back lifestyle. She attended art school and worked as an interior designer prior to opening deKor, a home goods boutique in LA's Echo Park neighborhood, finally realizing a lifelong dream. She eventually bought a second home in Ojai and decided to open another outpost of her shop there as well. Her passion for design, travel, and Southern California living now flourishes in both locations.

We met up with Isabelle and her two happy dogs at her charming Ojai home where she resides part-time with her husband, Brandon Boudet, and immediately added "second home in Ojai" to our wish list. We were taken with its vibrant mix of pattern, color, and texture, as well as its sophisticated, yet casual, sensibility. Warm sunshine, a glittering pool, and the mountainous backdrop only enhanced her distinctive, globally eclectic style. While waiting for the sun to fade into the hills for our last shot of the day, we chatted design and sipped white wine by the pool. Our delightful glimpse into deKor living left us with only one regret—we forgot to bring our swimsuits.

How did growing up in Sweden affect your design sensibility?

The Swedish have great design, so of course that played a role in my design sensibilities. I was also really affected by the lack of light in Sweden. It made me realize the importance of lighting a room to enhance the quality of life, especially during cold, dark winters. Not only did growing up in Sweden influence my design aesthetic, but it also motivated me to create beautiful spaces that elevate your mood, increase productivity, and instill a general sense of well-being.

How would you describe your style at home?

My style is globally eclectic. I grew up in Sweden, which is all about simple lines, a lot of white, open spaces, and working with light. My mother is a textile artist, so I'm very influenced by textiles, as well. That's where a lot of the global comes in, through rugs from Morocco and Turkey, and fabric from Africa. I also like things that are old, like farm tables, cabinets, and benches that have a lot of history. Mixing all that with a beautiful midcentury Danish armchair—that's eclectic global style. I'm not afraid of mixing different times and eras and textures. It all comes down to a feeling and, at the end, standing away from it and looking at it all like a painting.

Are there any similarities between styling a home and styling a store?

I always aspire for my stores to feel like a home—when you walk in, you want to linger, you want to stay. But obviously in a store, there's a lot of merchandising, so you style certain things to sell. In a home, on the other hand, you put out all the things you like, and then the last step is to edit. I feel strongly that a space should enhance your well-being, and for me that means less is more.

Styling comes from the gut. If you're styling a bookcase, you put your books in, then you move a few books so that some are laying down, some are standing up, and maybe you add a little ceramic pot. That's a spot where less might be more, a place where you can edit. You don't have to fit everything in there; sometimes it's nice to have a little bit of open space, because negative space gives you room to breathe. A home styled with a million things can look good, but once you sit in it you start to get a little crazy, a little overwhelmed. It's sensory overload.

What was your process for designing your Ojai home?

When we got this little house, my main focus was the outside. Since we are surrounded by nature, I wanted to do as much outdoor living as possible. The first thing I did was put the pool in, and then I worked my way out from there. I added a tent structure as a guesthouse, and we put a wood deck around the pool to fit with the feel of the rest of the house. Most farmhouses and summer homes in Sweden are red, so I paid homage to my roots by painting our house red with white trim. We moved our chickens up to Ojai, put in a vegetable garden, and built a pergola where my husband, a chef, put in a simple outdoor kitchen and cooking area. Inside the house, we took out the old floors and replaced them

with whitewashed wood flooring. We splurged on gorgeous tile in the kitchen, so to balance the budget, we simply repainted the existing cabinets. I wanted the entire home—both inside and out—to feel like a casual, warm place that you never want to leave.

What is your most cherished object in the home?

The wall hanging in the entryway that my mother, a textile artist, made and gave to me about eight years ago. It's a geometric piece, a type of Swedish kite, woven in a style called damask. It can be viewed from both the front and back, so you can hang it in the middle of the room. I have it displayed right when I walk into my little Ojai house. It's just beautiful and amazing, and because it's linen, the weaving is so fine. It's a work of art.

Your home has a cultural eclecticism that makes it hard to pinpoint any specific time or place, yet it still feels rooted. What does the mixing of cultures, styles, and time periods bring to your home?

It brings me contentment and happiness. Having things that remind me of trips, or having good colors or different cultures mixed in one space, makes me appreciate the world and human beings and helps me see the good in everything. If you have a kilim rug from Turkey and you pair it with a Danish chair, it just does something to your senses. It's interesting to not just go with the latest fad, and to add your own personality and meaning to your home with something from your family or from your travels. Don't be afraid of trying things.

"If you wake up in the
morning, and your home
feels good, it enhances your
happiness and makes you
kinder to people when you go
out in to the world."

SMALL SPACES

Smaller spaces can feel especially warm and cozy. With less room, each item chosen by the homeowner tends to be either highly utilitarian or deeply meaningful, and often both. These homes showcase how limited space can foster a purposeful and intentional focus on creating a welcoming setting that allows the people within them to live large.

CARL ANDRE · SCULPTURE AS PLACE · 1958–2010 · Dia · Yale

MELBOURNE NOW

Painting and Sculpture at The Museum of Modern Art · MoMA

The Age of Collage · gestalten

FRITZ KAHN · TASCHEN

JIM MARSHALL

all american

A NOTEBOOK AT RANDOM

PETER DOIG

Max Huber

William Kentridge

THE WORLD ATLAS OF WINE · 7TH

JAMES TURRELL · A RETROSPECTIVE · LACMA

Martin Parr

TIM NOBLE & SUE WEBSTER—WASTED YOUTH

Edition Stemmle

BACKYARD OASIS · The Swimming Pool in Southern California Photography

Gottfried Fliedl · Gustav Klimt · TASCHEN

Paul McCarthy

CHUCK CLOSE

SAFETY IN NUMBERS: NICK WAPLINGTON

BROKEN DREAM · KRATOCHVIL

You Owe Me A Feeling · Kunsth Berman Schmelling

Saul Leiter · Colors

William Eggleston

WILLIAM ALBERT ALLARD · PORTRAITS OF AMERICA

FIELD TRIP

CAI GUO-QIANG: I WANT TO BELIEVE

guy bourdin

HANDCRAFTED MODERN · AT HOME WITH MID-CENTURY DESIGNERS

TIBOR

ED RUSCHA

Photographers, Writers, and the American Scene · Visions of Passage · James L. Enyeart

Glitter and Doom: German Portraits from the 1920s

SIBUSISO MBHELE and his FISH HELICOPTER

OPERA DE PARIS

NOT A TOY

THE WRINKLES OF THE CITY · JR / José Parlá

MIKE KELLEY · ARENAS

KUSTOM BY EWEY NICKS

WINDOWS ON NATURE

CHRISTIANA COOP

Entrepreneur | Pattern Mixer | Co-Owner of Hygge & West

SAN FRANCISCO, CALIFORNIA

Aimee: It would be impossible to distill everything I love about Christiana into one paragraph. She's genuinely kind and cares deeply about friends and family. She's exceptionally stylish and has a particularly keen eye for art and statement necklaces. She's brilliantly funny, and we share an appreciation for sarcasm that has alienated more than one past boyfriend. But perhaps the best way to capture how I feel about her is to say that I consider her a sister, rather than a friend. We've been inseparable for the majority of our lives. Running a business together for the past ten years has added yet another dimension to our relationship, and we've managed, I think, to successfully navigate the potential pitfalls of mixing friendship and business. We celebrate our successes, support each other through our failures, and, at the end of the day, we've both decided that our friendship always takes priority.

When Christiana moved into her current apartment, I was so happy that she'd found such a sunny, character-filled space to call home. The working fireplace, original molding and built-ins, and clawfoot tub created the perfect canvas for her to build a very special, totally unique space. Christiana has always had the most wonderful eye for design, and it's been a joy to see her home evolve. I love this little jewel box of an apartment—there is always something new and interesting to discover. We've had so much fun here; whether we're entertaining a bunch of friends or just getting takeout and watching TV together, laughter is invariably part of the equation. One of the best things about our business is that I'm able to visit my dearest friend often, and I consider myself lucky to be able to spend so much time with her in her lovely home.

What was the design process for your home?

When I first moved into my little apartment, my idea was to keep things very minimal, which I thought would make it feel like a bigger space. But I quickly realized that's not actually how I live or like my space to feel, so I began to fill each room with pattern, color, art, and objects that make me smile. Red, pink, green, metallics, patterns, mirrors, marble, design books, ceramics, plants, art, throw blankets, and pillows—I love it all. The design of my home is constantly changing as we create new Hygge & West patterns that I want to try out, or as I experiment with new ways to use our wallpapers and textiles. For example, I initially had just wallpapered one accent wall in my bedroom with our Diamante wallpaper in gold. But after living with it for a few months, I decided that I wanted even more gold and glam, so I just went for it and wallpapered all four walls. A couple of years later, when we launched that same pattern in fabric by the yard, I made matching curtains. I didn't think I'd be into the concept of those two elements matching each other, but I like how it flows. The room now feels like a dark jewel box to me.

What does wallpaper bring to a home that other design elements can't?

Adding pattern to a wall can quickly and dramatically change the way a room feels and the story it tells. Because walls offer such a large, blank canvas, altering just that one element can have a huge impact in any space. I've switched up the wallpaper in my apartment more times than I (and my landlord) would care to admit, and every single time I'm happily surprised by what a difference it makes.

Life in a small apartment means wall space is limited. What are some creative ways you've come up with for creating more places to add pattern to your home?

Very few flat surfaces in my apartment have been overlooked for possible wallpaper applications. The back of my bathroom cabinet, my closets, my refrigerator, and the bottoms of drawers have all fallen prey to my wallpaper experimentation. Recently I wallpapered the inside of my kitchen cabinets with our Tassels pattern in black. It adds a festive element to my cocktail glasses collection.

What is your most cherished object in your home?

When I was graduating from law school and getting ready to move into a new apartment, I spent finals week scouring decor magazines and the mysterious Internet (yes, Google had just been invented) for inspiration. I realized then that this was my passion, which was unfortunate timing since I was getting a JD and not a degree in interior design. One of the magazine pages I dog-eared was a picture of a beautiful chair, the Sunset Chair by Christophe Pillet. I blew my entire first paycheck on it, and I remember the women who sold it to me saying I was "brave."

There was actually nothing brave about purchasing a piece of furniture I couldn't really afford, but five years later, when I decided to leave my legal career to pursue our business, I did finally feel that sense of bravery. The chair's shape is very contemporary and not something I'd likely choose now, but I'll always love it as a memento of discovering my passion and slowly finding the strength to pursue it.

You've managed to pack your place with style without it feeling cluttered and overwhelming.

I'm one of those people who really believe each and every thing has its designated space. So while I've admittedly packed a lot of things into my little home, they all have their place. It's "pretty stuff" versus "clutter," or at least to me it is. I recently removed everything but the books from the bookshelves in my living room. Only having books on those shelves made them almost textural instead of distracting, so the focus of that side of the room is really on the fireplace, where I keep my favorite crystal candlesticks and John Derian floral plates.

There's a ton of greenery in your apartment, which certainly contributes to its lush aesthetic. What role do plants play in your home?

Initially, I brought in a couple of plants as a way to fill in some empty spaces and add more life to my home. I didn't think I needed very many, as the patio that's visible just outside my window is quite lush. But over time, the plants became a hobby, and I really enjoy how there is now plenty of green from the outside reflected in.

What do you love most about your apartment?

It's one big pattern mix! I try to incorporate my favorite pattern from each of the collections we've launched, and each one evokes particular memories of the time period we were working on them. I made Julia Rothman's Foret fabric into curtains for my living room. That pattern was easily the most time-consuming and frustrating pattern we've ever created, due in part to our inexperience at the time with its delicacy and number of colors. I loved the pattern when Julia first showed it to us, and I appreciate it even more now after all the work that was put into transitioning it from a sketch, onto wallpaper, and then to fabric. The Ornate wallpaper designed in collaboration with Wit & Delight in my entry represents a huge transition in our company as we finally launched our bedding collection, of which that pattern is a part. The Diamante pattern was inspired by a trip Aimee and I took to Mexico City.

What is the biggest benefit of living in a small space?

You can have only so much in a small space, so it forces you to really think through each and every purchase—or at least it should. I'm still working on letting my small home dictate my shopping habits, I suppose. I spend so much time prop shopping for our photo shoots, scrolling through our wonderful design community's Instagram posts, and searching for pattern inspiration, that it can be very hard to resist buying things I don't

MAKING THE MOST OF EVERY SQUARE FOOT

"Treat the patio like its own room, even if it's a space you share with other people, by bringing out a patterned table-cloth, your favorite cocktail fixings, and special glassware. The patio is easily my favorite place to gather my boyfriend, his dogs, and close friends for a wine-soaked evening of good conversation and laughter. Even on cold nights, which there are plenty of here in San Francisco, we bundle up under cozy blankets, turn on the fairy lights, and spend hours outside under the stars, just chatting the night away."

technically need, but that strike me as exceptionally lovely. And I know that a bit more restraint with such purchases would be wise, especially given that I have next to no space left in my little place for anything new. But I can't help myself sometimes—there are just so many beautiful things out there.

What makes your home—and the life you live in it—hygge?

Living hygge is simply a state of mind. It's always there if you remember to look for it. For me, it's genuinely and deeply appreciating all the small moments I have at home and out in the world—that first cup of coffee in the morning snuggled in bed with my favorite guy and his dogs; relaxing with a good book in my beanbag chair while the sunshine streams in through a window; a drive along the coast with the windows rolled down, music flowing, destination unknown. And, most important, it's about the people who walk in the door. True happiness at home comes from being surrounded with people whom I love and can be completely myself around and who love me back—my friends, my family, and my boyfriend. A lively mix of pattern, a pretty plate collection, a book stack in just the right spot—all these things are just icing on the cake; albeit it delectable, delicious icing.

JULIA ROTHMAN

Illustrator | Author | Educator

BROOKLYN, NEW YORK

Hygge & West was not our first joint business venture—we actually started out as the first U.S. distributors of the Danish brand ferm LIVING. During that time, we had spotted a lovely illustration of birds and clouds online by Julia Rothman. Ferm asked us to test a custom wallpaper site they were experimenting with, so we got permission from Julia to use the image, uploaded it to the site, and a couple of weeks later, hung the resulting wallpaper in Christiana's kitchen. We immediately fell in love with it. Not long afterward, we decided that we wanted to start making our own wallpaper, and we knew exactly who our first artist would be. We met with Julia at ICFF (the International Contemporary Furniture Fair) in May of 2008, and by November of the same year, we launched Hygge & West. Daydream, as the bird pattern became known, was part of our first collection and continues to be a bestseller and the design people most associate with our brand.

We've continued to work with Julia over the years because she's an incredibly talented artist, and also because we thoroughly enjoy her. She has a wry sense of humor and is unfailingly honest. In the past eight years, Julia has gained a large, dedicated audience through her work as a magazine and newspaper illustrator, surface designer, and book author and illustrator, and we certainly feel indebted to her for helping our company grow and succeed. We know that we'll continue to collaborate in the future, if only so we can keep meeting with her to brainstorm new wallpaper patterns, catch up, and, of course, laugh.

What do you love most about pattern?

I like that it feels endless and mesmerizing, and that there's movement. I also like spaces to be filled. I'm not a huge fan of white space. When I was young, I had a small room, and my parents let me do what I wanted to it. I painted the walls bright yellow to replicate sunshine and had fuzzy wall-to-wall bright green carpet to mimic grass. I covered my entire dresser with stickers and drew all over my desk with Sharpies. As a teenager, I painted Keith Haring figures climbing up my wall. It was a cluttered, busy space, but I wouldn't mind having a room like that again.

Do you feel that your artistic style is similar to your style in interiors?

My drawings are a bit messy, cluttered, and use too many colors. I think I probably do the same thing in my apartment.

What's your process for coming up with a new pattern? How, if at all, is that process similar to designing your home?

When designing a new wallpaper, I'm thinking about other people. What is universally loved? What would people want to look at day after day? Could this fit in many different rooms? Then you have to think about how it's repeating and if there is anything your eye gets stuck on. Then the scale, and finally color. There are so many factors to get right. Once in a while, you hit a bull's-eye, but that's rare. It's a lot of work. On the other hand, designing my home isn't any work for me. I don't even think about it. I'm not someone who is consciously choosing items to match. I buy what I like and throw it in the mix. I'm not trying very hard, because it's my space for me. I don't need to make anyone else happy, which is a wonderful thing.

You've used Daydream in your kitchen. What inspired that pattern? What do you think it brings to the space?

I originally created this pattern for the lining of a coat. The coat company asked for something with birds and clouds, but they didn't like what I came up with. I worked really hard and was so bummed that it wasn't going to be used. I just put it in my portfolio as personal work. Then, when I met with Hygge & West about designing wallpaper, Christiana mentioned loving that design and wanting it in her own home, so we decided it would be in my first collection. I had no idea it would have this lasting effect. My rejected birds got a new life, and they soared. It's ridiculously cheesy to say, but I still feel tingles every time I see a new picture of it installed in a room, especially kids' rooms. It feels like validation.

Aside from it reminding me each morning of the personal meaning it has, this pattern just made sense in my kitchen. I've been in this rental for about five years. The rent is cheap and it's located right by Prospect Park, which is perfect for Rudy, my pooch. I have great restaurants nearby and many neighbor friends, so I've stayed. But the space is small and dark, and the kitchen is especially brutal: the window looks into the apartment next door, I don't have a dishwasher, and my broken refrigerator door is held closed with a magnet. I painted the cabinets white to brighten the room, but the wallpaper makes it a happier space and gives it some life.

You have a space in your home that you refer to as the "knickknack shelf." What type of objects do you display there?

That's true, but I say it slightly jokingly because they are not so much "knickknacks," which I think has a negative connotation. I buy a lot of art objects, as well as drawings and paintings. They used to be scattered around my apartment, but my boyfriend thought it was too messy, and they would often get in the way when he was doing something, like pulling a book off a shelf. So he put two shelves above the TV that are dedicated specifically to those things. There's a lot of pottery by friends, a small sculpture of a woman by Rachel Levit, some glove molds from Peru, and a pinecone my neighbor brought me after a trip Upstate. There was a time when these shelves got too filled, so I wound up scattering objects around again.

How do you separate work and home at the end of the day, even though both share the same space?

It's a real problem that I haven't actually solved. I work weird hours because I can. Sometimes I work in the living room while watching TV at night. When my assistant comes, he sits at my kitchen table. My work spills across many rooms. Right now, I am storing paintings in my bedroom closet behind my dresses.

What about your apartment makes it feel like home to you? What gives it its hygge-ness?

I like to keep things that remind me of something from my past. If I go on a trip, I like to buy something to have in my home to recall that memory. I think it's nice to fill your home with mementos of your life.

We love following your drawing sessions on Instagram, which often feature everyday scenes of your home, the friends and loved ones who visit you, or life in the city. What is it about these ordinary moments that feel meaningful to you?

Lately, my personal work has been about documenting a time and place. I will often go somewhere (a museum, a street corner, a fun event) and then come home later to make a record of it as a drawing. It's kind of like a diary. Some of those moments just happen to be someone coming over to draw, whether it's for a Ladies Drawing Night or just a friend watching a movie. It's relaxing for me to draw, so I do it whenever I can. Even if we are just sitting around in an ordinary moment, there are always things that can make my drawings unique. I particularly like drawing other people's homes and the stuff they have in them; it gives me a better idea of who they are. When you draw, you are very much studying everything, so it feels like personal research to sit and draw someone's home.

"Picking art is all about what you connect to. First, go to open studios— you get to meet the artist, which can be important. I've fallen in love with some drawings because I liked the artist so much that I wanted to have something of theirs. Also, look at illustrators. Illustrators get overlooked as 'artists' because they do a lot of commercial work, but sometimes that can be more beautiful or interesting. All illustrators do personal work, so when you see a drawing you like in a magazine or newspaper, look up the artist and contact them to see if they have work for sale."

KATIE RODGERS

Artist | Influencer | Dreamer
NEW YORK, NEW YORK

Little-known Hygge & West fact: Both of us took ballet lessons when we were young. We danced in the same garage dance studio in tiny White Rock, New Mexico, and dreamed of growing up to become ballerinas in New York City. That is, until we both hit an intense growth spurt around the fourth grade and were informed that neither of us had a "dancer's body." Nonetheless, ballet still captivates us, and when we happened upon Katie Rodgers's Instagram, with its glittering, graceful dancers, we were smitten.

Katie has been working as a full-time artist for about six years and does a mix of commissioned fine art paintings and full-scale creative collaborations with brands mostly in the fashion and beauty industry. We've had the pleasure of getting to know Katie and working on a small collection of wallpapers with her, and she is as sweet as she is talented. The first time we met in person, we chose the café in the basement of Bergdorf Goodman, which turned out to be the ideal setting. Katie was perfectly at home in that charming location, every inch of her a stylish New Yorker—so much so that we were surprised to learn that she's actually from a small town in Georgia. She, like us, grew up dreaming of dancers and New York, and in her character-filled apartment on the Upper East Side, she's made that dream a reality.

What story does your home tell?

I think my home tells a lot about me. I work from home, so a lot of my paints, palettes, and artwork are usually laying around or piled up on my desk area. So from that, you would know that I am an artist. You might know that I love classics and a bit of tradition from some of my furniture. And maybe you would learn that I love whimsical, fairy tale moments by the pirate ship hanging in my bedroom, my moon-phase garland, the mermaid, rabbit, and horses around my fireplace, and the sculpture of a nude woman lying on my mantel. I like to think that a lot of myself can be seen in the things within my home—especially if you look through my stack of books!

How is designing a home similar to composing a piece of art?

When I moved to New York, I viewed it as a fresh start, and a fresh canvas for my life and living space. I sold most of what I previously owned and wanted to slowly build my space. I did research online and saved spaces that inspired me. I became obsessed with interiors. I still am. I think a home is something that is always a personal work in progress. For a while, I thought, "When will I ever be finished with my apartment?" As the years have gone by, I've realized that my taste evolves with age and so does my home. Maybe it's just a simple change in throw pillows or wallpaper, but those little details can make a huge difference in a small space.

Your home has so many wonderful architectural elements—deep, oversize, shuttered windows, a gorgeous fireplace, and arched doorways, to name a few. How did you design your space with those elements in mind?

Those elements were the exact thing I was looking for when I sought out an apartment in New York. They give the space the quintessential old New York City look that I've always loved seeing in classic films. The great thing about a space like this is that you don't need to do too much to it because it already has so much character. I wanted to keep things fairly simple and just add a few key furniture pieces that related to the classic old-world charm, as well as a few modern elements to complement the vintage ones.

When I moved into my apartment, it was a scorching hot August day, but I knew as soon as fall and winter hit, I would love nothing more than to sit in front of that fireplace with a glass of wine. It really brings the place to life in the winter, and it's a great trick to get people out of hibernation when it's cold.

There's a beautiful eclecticism in your home—from your boldly patterned sofa to your collections of objects to your masterful mix of old and new— yet the whole space feels unified and cohesive.

I think a great way to build a cohesive space is to begin with a few key pieces and build from there. When I first moved in, I began with an heirloom settee and a drafting table that I knew I needed for my workspace. Then I slowly built around those pieces. I tied in classic and French-inspired pieces with a few modern updates here and there but kept them simple so they wouldn't compete with the vintage elements.

I also wanted to go with a classic color palette that played off the warm wood tones in the furniture. I thought I wanted a neutral, plain couch, but I found this great blue argyle Italian one at a small interior shop, and it just felt right, so I went for it. There's been a lot of trial and error over the years, but it always comes back to building around items I really love and cherish. One of the benefits of living in a small space is that it constantly forces you to edit yourself. You quickly learn what you love to surround yourself with every day, versus what you can live without. You learn to be more resourceful living in small spaces. Get rid of anything you don't find yourself using on a daily basis—you won't miss it, I promise!

You're one of the few lucky NYC dwellers who has nature outside your window instead of concrete and brick. How does that juxtaposition of city and nature influence the interior of your home?

It's the perfect mix. To go outside and immerse yourself in the bustling city of New York is so great, but to come home and relax surrounded by the peacefulness of nature outside your windows makes it that much better. There is one giant maple tree outside my window, and over the years I've noticed how much it affects the color of my space, even seasonally. In the spring and summer, my space is brighter and tinted with a green glow, and in the fall, it's the brightest yellow you can imagine. The winter is, of course, very gray and blue, but it's nice in its own way. I do love how that tree influences my space.

What are some of the ways you create hygge in your home?

I love the thought of hygge in a home. I believe in creating a home you feel great in—and especially a bedroom you feel wonderful waking up in. My home is very important for my mood in so many ways, especially because it's where I work, too. I've found that certain rituals help me turn my home into my office and back into my home during on and off hours, which keeps me sane during stressful work periods. When I'm not working in the evening, I usually light candles and put on the opposite kind of music of what I listen to while I'm working. It gets my mind out of work mode. I also love to hang prisms in the spring and summer to create little rainbow surprises on my walls in the afternoon. Those little things make a home more joyful.

What do you look for when choosing art for your space?

I am a wholehearted believer in purchasing art with a story. I don't think you should buy art just because it matches your color scheme. It could be a piece that you discover while you're traveling that holds a memory, or art that was created by a friend or family member. Art that comes with a story gives another dimension to the object beyond its physical presence. My grandparents lived overseas for a large part of their lives, and I love going to their home and hearing the stories about the objects and art they've collected. They don't own anything that doesn't have a story behind it, and I think that's really special. Their art is conversation.

"Make every square inch of space purposeful. It's much easier to make a small space feel like home—just a few bits of character go a long way."

KELLY SCHOEFFEL &
MATT MURPHY

Aimee: In a past life, I worked in marketing strategy for a major big-box retailer. My favorite thing about that job was having the opportunity to collaborate with some of the best advertising agencies in the world. I first met Kelly Schoeffel at a kickoff meeting with 72andSunny in their Los Angeles office. We both had just come back from trips to Mexico City, and we connected over our mutual love of strolling the streets of La Condesa and eating street tacos. I had the good fortune to work with Kelly for two years, during which time I came to consider her not just a colleague but a friend. She's brilliant and profoundly insightful, but more important, she's kind and funny. Basically, she's who I want to be when I grow up. Her husband, Matt Murphy, works with her at 72andSunny and is in every way her equal. Both are lovely people, unassuming, and humble, and they just happen to be two of the brightest stars in advertising today.

Their home epitomizes Southern California style—it's light and airy, and the outdoors blends seamlessly with the interior. The house is ideally located, within walking distance of all the amazing shops and restaurants Venice has to offer, but it also feels private and secluded. We fell in love with Kelly and Matt's dogs, Penny and Flash, and had so much fun catching up with the couple and recapping the day over several bottles of wine.

Your roles at work require constant creativity. How does that skill translate into creating a home?

Kelly: Creativity is a mindset, not an action or outcome. It's about embracing chaos, being open to trying new things, recognizing what excites you, and enjoying the journey. A home is never really done. But as a strategist, I do enjoy research, which is good and bad. It's good because I like to know what is out there before making a decision. But it's also bad because it can be hard to choose, or I often fall in love with things I cannot afford and then pine for them, sometimes for years.

Matt: Your home needs to slow you down and help recharge your spirit. I take pride in surrounding myself with art and books and objects that inspire me. Regardless of what project I'm working on, pulling out a great book and seeing inside another artist's mind always gives me something to feed off of.

How do you find or create hygge in your life?

Kelly: To me, hygge is about creating conditions for happiness and love. And to that end, our world is very sensory—we love being surrounded by beautiful and thought-provoking art; food that's bright, fresh, and flavorful; and spaces that ooze hospitality and draw people in. We don't need a lot of things, but we want the things in our lives to matter, and to have a distinct and meaningful role. You need to follow your gut, but also be mindful in your choices.

How does the home influence the way you live in it?

We chose this home for its beauty but also its efficiency, which manifests in our lifestyle and values. Big windows looking out on lush California gardens mean there is always light and a connection with nature. A smart, European kitchen at the heart of our home ensures we're always gathering around delicious smells and tastes. An overall sense of Eastern minimalism means we need to keep organized—we have a lot of beloved objects, including countless art books, but not a lot of clutter or even a television. This house demands a balance of pleasure and restraint and our lives are better for it. And it's small, which is good because we like to be together instead of hiding in opposite corners of the home.

If one's home is a reflection of their personal brand, how would you describe your brand?

Kelly: Aspirationally, I'd like to say "spontaneous harmony"—lively, yet peaceful; warm and inviting, but never sentimental; a bit hedonistic, yet restrained. Definitely a contradiction, but it works.

Matt: My drawing teacher at RISD [Rhode Island School of Design] used a phrase to describe his way of seeing the world: "Partially rendered and partially contour." The goal is to fill in enough details to make your vision clear, but leave enough room for magic and mystery to fill in the rest. I think how we go about designing our life conforms to this logic.

How do you create and embrace coziness in your home?

Kelly: Lots of light, lots of plants, lots of pets (two is our magic number). But my biggest no-duh advice is to literally keep it cozy—don't have more space than you need, or it will inevitably fill with junk or a feeling of emptiness, both of which suck energy instead of giving it. I love a small space. I love everyone in eyesight or earshot of one another.

Your outdoor space seems to function as an additional room to your home, rather than a yard. What do you like best about it?

Our outdoor space is so alive and full of life—from the textures of cacti to the smells of flowers and trees to the sounds of hummingbirds and mourning doves. We feel so lucky to be surrounded by this beautiful cacophony.

We love how you've stacked books on the floor to showcase your collection, but also created additional display space for art and other objects.

Stacks of books can be used for anything, and we've done it all—bedside tables, table bases, stools. The only downside is it's harder to enjoy the books themselves, so we're slowly getting on board with the idea of bookshelves. One of our space-saving tricks is to give objects a home. It can be in a pile, but let it be intentional.

What's your favorite time of day in the house?

Kelly: I'd say around seven or eight o'clock in the morning, even though it is not the brightest or most golden hour. But rays of sun begin to creep over the fence and trickle through the trees, and we are reminded that we're lucky enough to live in California. That feeling never gets old.

"It's a cliché, but you have to buy art that you love. That said, you cannot love what you do not know, so you have to become a student of art, or have a trusted friend or advisor who can guide you. We do see art as an investment, and it's important to understand its value and the cultural forces that will affect it in the future—for example, how past work has appreciated, whether the artist has a big show coming up, etc."

FAMILY

Ask anyone what they love most about their home, and they're likely to tell you it's the people with whom they share it. These homes focus on spaces dedicated to gathering and connecting with loved ones, and the style that emerges from places meant to be shared and enjoyed while in the company of others.

ROD HIPSKIND

Stylist | Entrepreneur | Co-Owner of Perish Trust

OAKLAND, CALIFORNIA

Christiana: I met Rod Hipskind more than a decade ago during a chance encounter at Eden & Eden, a shop owned and operated by our mutual friend Rachel Eden. Shortly after, Rod and his business partner, Kelly Ishikawa, opened the Perish Trust, and I became an instant admirer. I loved everything about it—the space was dark, intriguing, charming, and brimming with unique vintage finds displayed in the most creative ways. Walking through it felt like embarking on a treasure hunt. After purchasing an iron mouse candlestick holder on the store's opening night, I would stop in every now and then to see what new vintage pieces Rod and Kelly had found, and I always enjoyed chatting with Rod about his shop, styling work, and life in general.

When thinking about who we might want to feature in this book from Northern California, Rod's name immediately came to mind. We knew that he'd be a pleasure to interview, and that we might even learn a thing or two observing such a skilled, highly regarded stylist at work in his own home. We also guessed that his home that he shares with his partner, Andres Power, and daughter, Inez, would be picture perfect. We were right on all counts.

What was the process of creating your home like?

When Andres and I found this home, it was begging for some love. All the elements of a 1906 Edwardian were there, but they were hiding. We both felt like these amazing architectural elements wanted to shine. The previous owner, who I am certain had the best of intentions, had tried in earnest to apply a mid-twentieth-century eye to the house by covering its details. A utilitarian streamlining, if you will. We spent the better part of our first year trying to reverse that process and highlight its originality. We also tried our best to apply a lens of today's modernity by keeping our choices simple and unified with color and finishes. Although the house will probably never be completed in our minds, I am most proud of just doing the work we have done while being respectful of the home's heritage.

There's a beautiful play of pattern and texture throughout your home. What do you think those two elements bring to a space?

It's that deep desire for authenticity again. We both love to travel, and we are constantly adding our finds from near and far to our permanent collection. I think that curating a home shouldn't be difficult. Use the things you love, and surprise yourself by mixing those things together. Combining prints and textures works best when there's neutrality of color in the bones of a space.

How do you decide when to buy old and when to go new?

More often than not, I go old, mostly due to the fact that I was raised scouring flea markets and collecting antiques, and so I feel most at home with them. But there is something to be said about a modern and clean space to unify all of your collected goods. We obviously don't have a modern space, but we have done our best to create a very neutral palette to display our favorite finds. I mostly go new when something is a utilitarian object, such as a plate, a sofa, or bedding.

In designing your home with Andres, did you learn any tips or tricks for how to work together to create a meaningful, well-styled space that feels cozy and welcoming to both of you?

Independent of each other, we are both homebodies. We demand a sanctuary to come home to—a respite from the commute, our jobs, politics, etc. I don't think our desires are out of the ordinary. Honestly, it's the basic equation—comfortable and realistic furniture, good textures in textiles, nice bedding, a dog, some wine, and a record player. The rest is just fluff, pretty things that aren't too precious.

You recently added a beautiful baby girl, Inez, to your family. How did you design her room so that it felt like a child's space but still reflected your personal style?

We made a conscious effort when we started her room to just add her and the things she or we might need. A lot of what's in Inez's room is stuff we already had in our guest room, and we used our baby goggles to add punches of color through objects and textiles. I love the excuse to add whimsy and fun to a kid's room. We want to foster her imagination from the get-go. Inez has changed us irrevocably. I see everything differently now. The whole hue of the universe has changed.

Designing with family in mind can present both obstacles and opportunities. Which, if any, did you run into and how did you work with or around them?

The biggest challenge in our home is space. With baby comes loads of stuff, and our house is just a bit over one thousand square feet. We spent a lot of time reorganizing closets and reinventing Ikea plug-and-play closet organizers. We also tried to locate dead space in the house and install shelving and, most importantly, a large built-in closet with a bench in our foyer. It's the smartest thing we could have done. It allows us to stow away arriving parcels and all of Inez's dailies: diapers, diaper bag, formula, Ergo, toys, etc. Our "dad" jackets and bags live there, too. I have a strange fascination with mudrooms, and the foyer is like a mudroom behind doors. It's expansive, practical, and hides all that I don't want to see on a regular basis. There is something so satisfying in dealing with a smaller space. You must think creatively about the way you use it, and when you have done it right, there is such a sense of satisfaction in using only what you need.

How do you add personality and meaning to your home?

You must add antiques, vintage, and handcrafted items. There is no alternative to the depth that these things can bring. Also, don't be afraid of what you love. Nothing adds personality and character more than the things you love. It's your home, not anyone else's.

CREATING GIFTS WITH MEANING

"The patchwork blanket *(at right)* was a gift from my dearest friend and business partner, Kelly Ishikawa. She asked all the guests attending our baby shower to contribute a scrap of fabric and then asked our friend, artist Matt Katsaros, to construct a baby quilt from them. It's a very special—and practical—gift."

Are there any traditions you maintain in this home?

We both were lucky enough to come from homes where cooking was status quo. Andres and I had grandmothers who spent a lot of time in the kitchen, and we both paid attention. Many of those recipes (mostly remembered, not written down) pop up in our kitchen. Cooking is a simple joy that can be meditative for us. There is such an inherent creativity in the kitchen.

What's your favorite time of year in your home?

I like this house best in the autumn. I seem to like the whole world best in the autumn, when it's like living in an Andrew Wyeth painting. It's a time to reflect and turn toward oneself, to take a breath. There's a balance I enjoy in the fall of Northern California; remnants of summer's glory are still everywhere, but the nights get cooler, the days shorter, and there's the promise of rain. Autumn and the concept of hygge seem synonymous to me.

Are there any home design rules you always follow? Any that you often break?

One to follow: neutral walls and architectural details. One to break: neutral walls and architectural details. And design does not always have to be expensive. Don't let anybody tell you otherwise.

KRISTIN HOLLANDER

Entrepreneur | Creative | Mother

MINNEAPOLIS, MINNESOTA

Aimee: I met Kristin Hollander through mutual friends when she was pregnant with her daughter, Elee, and felt an instant connection with her. Kris is one of those women the rest of us look at and wonder how she does it—she's the co-owner of a successful creative agency, a great mom to her adorable children, a loyal friend, and the most stylish person I know (and her husband, Jeff, is funny, smart, and the second most stylish person I know.) Kristin and Christiana have also become close friends, and the three of us are notorious for nights when "one quick glass of wine" stretches into hours' and bottles' worth of stories and laughter.

After having completely remodeled an adorable foursquare in Minneapolis's Uptown neighborhood, Kris and Jeff realized that their family of four had outgrown the house. They found their current home in Lowry Hill and set out on another extensive remodel. The result is stunning—a seamless blend of the character and detail of an old home with their impeccable taste in modern decor. It also feels unquestionably like the family home it is. We love spending time in that beautiful, warm house with our beautiful, warm friends.

What was it like designing your home?

When we purchased this home, it was a fixer-upper; pretty much every surface had to be touched. We wanted it to reflect our love of modern design, while also maintaining the integrity of the spaces of a one-hundred-plus-year-old home. We feel like we are still in the process of designing our home, and always looking for interesting pieces, old and new. The living room was our biggest challenge. It's long and has two seating areas. We struggled to figure out a way to create two spaces that would be comfortable, both for family and entertaining, and I think we finally landed on a good solution for the room.

Your home's mostly black-and-white color palette sets the stage for the bold shapes and lines of your lighting, furniture, or other accents. What motivated the decision to add interest with form rather than color?

To Jeff and me, white on white is the perfect palette—clean and modern. We thought keeping the color scheme understated and letting the natural light and accents do all the work would be interesting. We also choose items that feel masculine or feminine—when you juxtapose those traits, it somehow always works.

Although you've kept the palette minimal, you've managed to create a wonderful sense of depth, texture, and interest in your house. What are the key ingredients to making a monochromatic space come alive?

Layers! I love layering pieces. We don't take a lot of risk with color, so using different shapes and textures helps add interest on a shelf or in a corner.

Although your home has a distinctly contemporary feel, it also seamlessly incorporates more traditional elements, like decorative molding and wall paneling.

Jeff and I absolutely love classic French apartment design and decor. The French are masters at combining the stately, ornate appearance of Parisian apartments with modern furniture and objects with minimal lines. The space should do all the heavy lifting and look just as great empty. We don't have the kind of restraint that French designers do because, hey, we're American!

While most of your home has white walls, you decided to paint one room entirely in gunmetal gray—trim and all.

We wanted to do something unexpected in that space as a point of departure from the neutral base we'd established throughout the house. Our designer friend showed us some monochromatic looks that we liked, but we thought they were too intense. We decided to go for it, but we used a slightly warm gray to soften the intensity a bit. We didn't want the room to feel too dark or heavy, so we added a touch of green and pink to brighten the room and create balance.

"People with families have to be
honest with themselves about how they
will use their home, and then design to
complement their lifestyle."

You and your husband have two beautiful children. How did you create a home that is both design forward and family friendly?

If you love design and you're not careful, you could end up with an impeccably styled home that your kids are miserable in. For example, we don't like having the television as a focal point in the main room, or, even worse, having all the furniture oriented toward it. But at the same time, we spend the most time in that room snuggled up on the sectional with the kids, so we had to compromise our aesthetic preferences.

Chairs in the kitchen are a must. People always hang out in the kitchen, so give them a place to sit down. When we remodeled, we knew we wanted an overhang on the counter-top for exactly this reason. And it gives us a quick and easy place to feed the kids breakfast on school days. We agonized a bit over the upstairs, but finally turned a small bedroom, which was probably a nursery, into a closet. We also turned a tiny bathroom into a laundry room and turned the huge, existing closet into a large bathroom. Now the upstairs works perfectly for our day-to-day life and we can't imagine it any other way. You just have to consider how you will actually live in the space and the decisions become easy.

What do you love most about your home?

I love that when I look around at our objects, I'm reminded of where we found each one. Jeff and I are really into thrifting and antiquing, and we only purchase things that we love. When you have a connection with an item, it doesn't matter if it fits perfectly because you will find a place for it. It's a little memento of the place where you found it and the enjoyment you had that day; it's more than decor, it's a memory. All these pieces have little stories of their own that make you feel something. My husband is drawn to intense objects that sometimes evoke a sense of sadness, especially religious artifacts. I'm drawn to playful objects that make me smile. So when we combine these influences, they create a sense of visual tension that we find really interesting. We love everything in our home because it all has been intentionally and thoughtfully collected.

How do you create or find hygge in your everyday life? How does your home factor in?

We love to host family and friends. When we first saw the house, we could envision how all the spaces would work for future entertaining, and it's one of the reasons we decided to buy it. Our home functions well for our family every day, with a sense of comfort and warmth, but we're lucky that the space is also versatile and can accommodate larger gatherings. However, when I see my family relaxing in the living room before bedtime, with our kids snuggling with our dog on the floor, that's when the feeling of hygge really sets in. Small moments like those are my favorite.

4 - 1964 - HAYWARD GALLERY EXHIBITION - SEPTEMBER 1992

RACHEL BEHAR

Artist | Mother | Orchardist
SEBASTOPOL, CALIFORNIA

Christiana: When Rachel Behar was first starting her organic baby clothing company, speesees, she needed help with her trademark. A lawyer at the time, I volunteered to help her through our firm's pro bono program. She confidently walked into the conference room in a vintage floral top and dangling gold earrings, carrying colorful sketches of adorable animals on tiny, colorful clothing. I desperately wanted to trade my yellow legal pad for her sweet little notebook full of dainty doodles and big ideas.

Over the years, as her business grew, she became a wonderful friend of mine. Not only was she a huge inspiration and motivating force behind my decision to eventually leave law firm life behind to step into the design world, but also an invaluable mentor and an encouraging voice in the often overwhelming realm of self-employment. Visiting her at her serene home, now surrounded by apple trees and two bright-eyed, beautiful children, I couldn't be happier to see where she's planted her family's roots. Her five-acre apple orchard has all the ingredients to nurture a healthy, happy, and art-filled life. I can't wait to see what delights await Rachel, her husband, Justin, and their children as they weed-wack, clean, pick, build, paint, and gather their life ahead.

You recently left Marin County behind for a little more leg room on an apple orchard in Sebastopol. What has the transition from urban to rural life been like?

Dare I say, easy? I grew up attending a ranch camp every summer of my childhood, where I was immersed in farm life, and my dream was to re-create this for my children. This camp was one of the inspirations for speesees, the organic cotton baby clothing company I created and ran for nearly a decade in San Francisco. When Justin and I met, we pretty quickly realized that while we were energized by city life, we yearned for a quieter, simpler life in the country. We got married in Occidental, California—a spot we discovered when we first starting dating—and we were committed to finding our future land in that neighborhood. Three years later, we found our spot, which we named A&A Apple Farm after our children, Aidan and Adeline. We love the space and quietude of country life. Aside from the fox family that frequently parties on our deck and keeps us up at night, Sebastopol has given us a warm welcome.

How would you describe the style of your home?

Eclectic modern farmhouse. We like to mix it up. The design of our home is always in flux and is really a combination of myriad styles. Vintage, rustic, bohemian, midcentury modern, and farmhouse style—anything goes! I think classic farmhouse staples nicely complement modern pieces and can almost take on a modern feel themselves. Usually I am a color girl, but I found that painting the walls white made it easier to commingle aesthetics and styles. Whatever you choose to do together is your own work of art.

How has life as a mom influenced the way you design and decorate your home? In what ways have you made your house family friendly, but also design forward?

Form follows function. Less is more. The spaciousness in the house allows for the kids to move around without knocking things over. Fewer books on their bookshelf means fewer books on the floor (and fewer books for Mommy to constantly tidy). I like to keep most of their stuff in baskets in their rooms, and they have special drawers in the kitchen where they can take out their own dishes. Shoes and backpacks live in the mudroom, thank you very much. I try to integrate the kids' pieces into the decor, like their rocking horse, which has a place in the living room. Also, things can't be too precious. I'm always thinking of ways to include the kids in the design of our home and make it easy for them to interact with the space. But most of all, I just send them outside to play!

What are some of your favorite ways to use wallpaper and pattern?

I love to use wallpaper as a splash or peekaboo pattern. Our master bathroom is rustic, with its reclaimed wood wall and black tile floor and shower, but when you slide open the water closet door, surprise! There's a modern wallpaper. That makes me happy.

Art has been a big part of your life, from your days at art school, to your time as founder of speesees, to today. How is your affinity and eye for art reflected in your home?

I see art everywhere. Beautiful art and design make me happy, from the typeface on a vintage Band-Aid container to the vintage rug beneath our bed that Justin got while he was in Turkey (my grandfather picked up the other two rugs during his travels as a naval admiral). When Justin and I first started dating, I realized that we have a similar aesthetic. We painted the artwork above the bed ourselves using paint samples we had left from our living room in our first house. Justin painted this great red shape first, so we decided to paint the rest of the canvas white to make it prominent. We call it Mr. Fishbird. We also have several paintings by Anne Faith Nicholls in the house, along with outsider art from Creativity Explored in San Francisco. Artwork imbues story, emotion, and history. You can see the hand that created it, which draws one in and connects us on a deeper level. I see the wallpaper as art, pillows as art, wood walls as art, imperfect shelving as art. I love to envision the farm being one big (imperfect) piece of art.

What is hygge for you?

Hygge is natural light, record players, linen sheets, wallpaper, apple crates, digging in the dirt, playing guitar, sheepskins, simple fixtures, whitewashed floors, vintage books, Edison bulbs, white dishes, fresh flowers, apple trees, reclaimed wood, an old typewriter, kilim pillows, hot baths, soft pillows, adirondack chairs, and, of course, a dog. Can a dog be hygge? We are getting a dog!

We plan to grow into our name and actually become a farm in the years to come. And while the design process will be ever evolving, one thing's for certain: we will be keeping it hygge.

CREATING SPACES FOR EVERYONE

"Kids need space to play and adults need space to breathe, so we aimed to make the house spacious for everyone. A chalkboard is always useful in a bedroom or play space (or mudroom), and I am always a fan of a black wall. Pops of color and pattern are always fun, too. I created a bookshelf by attaching wallpapered plywood to the back of an IKEA shelf. The playful pattern of the wallpaper creates a sweet backdrop for the kids' books, objects, and baskets of toys. I also like to display vintage children's pieces like my dad's Swedish red horse and a Brio red rolling egg toy that was mine as a child."

JULIE BACKER

Wallpaper Enthusiast | Mother | Farmer

HUGO, MINNESOTA

Aimee: I met Julie Backer through work many years ago. She was part of the very first team I worked on, and I quickly gravitated toward her generous personality and infectious laugh. Julie's easy smile and impeccable fashion sense immediately make an impression on everyone who meets her. She is always full of funny stories about her life and family, and is known for being an exceptional hostess who regularly throws dinners and parties that inevitably last for days because no one wants them to end.

When Julie decided to move out of Minneapolis to the family farm where she grew up, I couldn't wait to see her new home and the lifestyle it would beget. If you know Julie, you wouldn't necessarily expect her to live on a farm—she's a frequent traveler to Los Angeles and New York City and fits into those urban environments extremely well. But when we arrived, it quickly became obvious that this was the perfect spot for her, her husband, Brigg, and their two daughters, Eloise and Georgia. The girls gave us a quick tour before Julie arrived, introducing us to all the family pets and telling us about the myriad fun activities they are able to partake in at their new home. The farm exudes the same warm charm of its owners, and you just can't help but feel welcome there.

You recently sold your home in Minneapolis and moved into a farmhouse outside the city. What motivated that decision?

This was originally my parents' home. As the youngest child of five, I was the only one that grew up at the farm, but three of us got married here, and nearly all of us moved into the guest house, or "the cabin," at one life juncture or another.

When my ninety-two-year-old dad was tired of his failing body, he decided it was time to go, so he stopped eating. My five siblings, their five spouses, their collective eighteen children, and the five great-grandchildren—our whole family—came out to the farm and stayed day in and day out until the end. Friends delivered fabulous meals, and the bottles of wine and scotch overflowed from the recycling bin.

In the daytime, we carried my dad out to the porch to watch us play badminton, or out on the lawn under the windmill to teach us our last tennis lesson. At night, we sat around the fire pit or piled onto his bed to record him telling stories about his time as the owner of Crescent Creamery, the war, and life running the Commodore Hotel. As he got weaker, we would all fall asleep to my mom singing "You Are My Sunshine" to him. The music never stopped and the fire pit never went out for those six days.

I am spontaneous to a fault. When I have an idea, I rarely think of the how, and never, ever entertain the what-ifs. Looking back, I guess it was simply too hard to say good-bye to my dad and the special place he created with my mom for all of us kids.

What do you love most about living in the country?

I love so much, I don't know where to begin. For me, it was more about moving home to carry on my parents' dream of creating a beautiful place for family, friends, family of friends, and friends of family to get together, rain or shine, and have a ball. The magical childhood was a by-product. However, one thing that very much surprised me when we settled in was that I didn't realize the bubble we had lived in and the narrow view of diversity I had. I have met so many people from so many backgrounds, and I am so grateful for the village I have come to know here.

How has the country setting influenced the way you've designed and decorated your home?

I do feel some responsibility to honor the farmhouse it has been these last two hundred years, and preserve some of the folksiness and early American treasures my mom collected because they would be out of place anywhere else. It's their home, too.

What does wallpaper bring to your home that paint, art, and other decor can't?

When we first moved in, we were prepping the bedroom walls upstairs for new wallpaper. Jane, our master wallpaper hanger, slowly steamed away layer after layer of different papers (a messy, hot, humid job). These were papers my mother had hung throughout her

forty-plus years in this home. Some patterns I hadn't seen since I was a little child, but I remembered each and every one of them. Those patterns stick with you in a nostalgic way, like hearing a Led Zeppelin song and being transported back to a kegger on the banks of the Mississippi. Someday I'll be the one adding the wallpaper layers, and my kids can peel back the memories.

Your home, with its beautiful spaces and plethora of ways to enjoy the outdoors, seems like the perfect place to grow up. What do you think a childhood in the country can offer your daughters that life elsewhere can't?

By no means does it come without trade-offs—it certainly does—but my kids have endless freedom to explore. They run barefoot everywhere: tall grass, swamps, rocky roads, barnyards. They have learned what plants are itchy, where the snakes live, and where the snapping turtles travel each spring to lay their eggs.

In me, too, the farm fuels a sense of fearlessness and comfort in being outside with all the critters, big or little, day or night, snow or heat. We hear symphonies at night that are the most beautiful sounds. And as spring turns to summer, summer to fall, it's a new concert. The peepers become bullfrogs; the sandhill cranes migrate through. I like that this place has given my family more intrigue and respect for all the living things around us, and we've cut down on screen time without even trying.

It's not just the wild animals that came with country living—you've created quite the menagerie of domestic ones, too.

When we moved to the farm our family multiplied in size, and continues to do so. We arrived with two parakeets, who were quickly joined by Midnight, the three-week-old oil-soaked kitten we found in an old tire; Dollie, who was a rescue dog from Alabama; a rabbit; twenty chickens; and two absolutely hilarious goats, Winnie and Annie, that are sure to entertain at every cocktail party. Each animal has its own oddball personality that we know and love. We've come to depend on them for companionship and sometimes food, in that order. The kids have the responsibility of keeping them healthy, from giving the goats shots and trimming their hooves, to daily feedings.

UNEXPECTED WALLPAPERING

Using a vibrant wallpaper to line the insides of kitchen cabinets adds a fun pop of color and pattern to a normally unadorned space. It also emphasizes the beauty of everyday objects, elevating and transforming a simple collection of glassware and dinnerware into a lovely display. Wallpapered stairs are not just the perfect use for wallpaper remnants, but they also add a unique and lively dose of fun to an oftentimes neglected design element.

VIOLA ROUHANI

Architect | Mother | Nature Enthusiast
BRIDGEHAMPTON, NEW YORK

Christiana: I met Viola Rouhani through a mutual friend and was intrigued by her Scandinavian background, given our company's name and my admiration for Scandinavian design. Her childhood in Denmark and Sweden, spent surrounded by nature, playing in the forests, going berry-picking and fishing in the summers, and sledding and ice skating in the winters, sounded nothing short of magical.

Nature still has a huge impact on her. A partner in an architectural firm based in Bridgehampton, New York, Viola specializes in high-end, modern residential architecture, where she takes her cues from the beauty of each home's natural surroundings. I have always been fascinated by listening to her speak about architecture, every material, angle, and view so well thought out, and I'd often wondered what her personal family home would be like. Her deliberate and thoughtful approach to design and unique viewpoint on what makes a house a home made her an obvious choice for this book. It was such a pleasure to visit her, her husband, Paul, and their son, Julian, at their design-forward and family-centric home. We only hope we didn't overstay our welcome—their warmth and humor, the salty white surf, and the sparkling beach made it difficult to say our good-byes.

What inspires you, both in your work and your home?

Trying to find an "inevitable solution" is something that is important to me. I think the best buildings are those that don't feel forced—everything has a place, nothing jumps out, and there are no visual disruptions. I like places to flow naturally; proportion and light are quite important in this regard. A strong connection to the exterior is also important, as is a sense of enclosure. I like the idea of the progression of starting more cocooned, then opening up to a view, and ending in the moment when you are outside in that view.

Your firm specializes in high-end architecture. How does your work influence your own home and aesthetic?

Designing houses for others is different only in that it's a dialogue with someone outside yourself. Every project is a custom house for that person, on that particular site, and with that budget. My own house is a small addition and renovation, so it's a very different story in some ways. But in other ways, it's exactly the same: how to optimize the space you're creating in terms of light, orientation, and flow. There's the outside, which is a natural, soft, and beautiful place, and then there's the architecture, which is more regimented and in contrast to the landscape. They meet again in terms of materials—siding is often left to weather naturally, blending into its surroundings over time. Large openings bring in light and give you the indoor-outdoor connection.

How would you describe your personal style?

I believe in clean lines and well-proportioned neutral spaces. I tend to deviate personally with how the spaces are filled, however. My own sensibility often differs from clients' in that I like the tension of something being out of proportion, or being more whimsical within a neutral space.

What are your tips for homeowners who want to create a high-end look at home but don't have the budget for it?

Mix and match. There's nothing wrong with getting items from IKEA or other similar retailers, as long as you pick wisely and balance them against higher-value pieces.

What is one element that homeowners should always invest in to create a luxe home?

A nice sofa goes a long way.

Much of your work—and your own home—complements and speaks to its surrounding environment. Why is that important?

We happen to live in an amazingly beautiful place—to not bring this into your home, or have your home be the perch from which you enjoy it, is a real lost opportunity. We should take advantage of it, and I do encourage clients to engage with it through design as much as possible. This doesn't mean you have to have a window facing every great view, though. There still has to be enclosure so that when you do have the opportunity to engage, it has meaning.

ESSENTIAL ART
50 YEARS
OF JANUS

Having a family often comes with a lot of clutter. How are you able to maintain a clean, stylish aesthetic, while still housing all the things having a son entails?

We're lucky to have a child who appreciates our aesthetic. Pretty early on, a clear directive was given that the main part of the house should remain as clutter-free as possible, while other places in the house, such as the basement or the yard, are where true experiments can take place. We also have the accessory structure in the back, which has functioned as everything from a painting studio to a pretend schoolhouse, and, most recently, a Dungeons & Dragons' lair. In this regard, there has never been a lack of places to make a true mess. It just doesn't have to be where we eat and live. I think it's really important that children be given the opportunity to explore things and be creative. With Paul being a scientist, and me having grown up with scientist parents, we are always encouraging Julian to be curious. From an early age, he's been given a slew of objects such as old VCRs, radios, and clocks to take apart and tinker with. Most of this happens below the main floor.

Clean, minimalist design is deceptive in that it's far from simple to do well. How do you edit your home and what tips do you have for others who want to do the same?

You have to be really disciplined about clutter. White walls help, of course. We have a rule at our house: if you bring something new in, something old has to go. It's hard to stick to; I'm constantly trying to get rid of things. I made a decision at a very young age that I would not get emotionally attached to physical objects, perhaps because I've been surrounded by so many of them my whole life. I've tried to stand by this, but understandably it is hard when there are so many memories associated with certain things. My son is super nostalgic—he loves collecting things, so I'm not allowed to get rid of too much.

Home is an incredibly personal space, filled with meaning. How do you create a meaningful home that feels true to who you are?

I'm surrounded by furniture and objects that either came from my parents or my husband's parents, that we've collected on trips, or that have been made by friends or us. Everything in our house has a story.

How do you create contentment within your home?

First of all, the house has to be clean and uncluttered. Must-haves for me are a lot of daylight and open spaces. At the same time, there needs to be areas that provide enclosure and a place to retreat. Ideally, there is a strong connection to the outside, whether visually or physically, but it has to be orchestrated correctly—one solution does not fit all. And while it may sound unromantic, it's important to me that a house is easy to maintain. It shouldn't be so precious that you're afraid to really use it. It's not a museum; it's a home— it's meant to be lived in.

GEMMA van der SWAAGH

Interior Designer | Wallpaper Enthusiast | Mother

CONCORD, MASSACHUSETTS

Gemma van der Swaagh is someone who also left the corporate world behind to pursue her passion, so we felt a genuine kinship with her from the very first time we met her. When her oldest, Callum, was born, Gemma made the decision to leave her job to stay home with him; two more sons, Ewan and Graham, soon followed. This can be a difficult choice for a mother, but for Gemma it was simple. She loves being home with her kids, even though at times it is far more work than a day at the office ever was. But more important, she felt that this life would be more fulfilling for both her, her husband, Seth, and her family. Taking time to be home with her kids also gave Gemma the opportunity to pursue an old passion—interior design. She started taking classes at Rhode Island School of Design for a formal education in the theory of design, and then started her own interior design business.

It is her own home that perhaps best showcases Gemma's talent. Filled with bright, eye-catching patterns, original art, and an abundance of books (not to mention toys), each room is thoughtfully designed, yet brimming with life. From the moment we pulled up to her home and saw her waving to her oldest son as he hopped on the school bus, to our good-byes over a skillfully made French 75, there was a pervasive feeling of love and family throughout Gemma's home.

How would you describe your aesthetic?

I think of my design aesthetic as clean and crisp, but always inviting, relaxed, and livable. I like simple shapes, but I use color, textures, and layers to add elements of interest and fun. We spend so much time in our houses, but too often we don't actually experience our homes. I believe interior design should make you feel something and shift your time at home from purely passive, to something slightly experiential and emotive. It shouldn't get in the way of living, but it should augment it by inviting you in and helping you relax, enjoy, and maybe even smile.

What was the design process for your home like?

We had lived in our house for less than a year when our five-year-old son was unexpectedly diagnosed with an aggressive form of leukemia. At that time, the house wasn't particularly done, and suddenly I wasn't home for the six months that he lived at the hospital. As a result, nothing progressed in terms of the design. His hospital stay was a very hard time for him and our family, and to take my mind off things, I would spend time at night when he was asleep planning what I would do with the house when we got out of there. I promised myself that I would make the house a beautiful refuge that we could all enjoy together.

The culmination of our son's treatment was a bone marrow transplant, which required him to be in isolation once he left the hospital. This meant that he (and my other children) couldn't go to school or go out in public spaces for about nine months. During that time, I worked hard to create a relaxing, inviting, cozy, and beautiful environment for our family to live in. The biggest challenge was obviously that I wasn't able to leave the house with the kids or allow anyone to enter the house, and I needed to continue to care for our sons throughout the process. But I was proud to succeed at creating a warm and comforting space for our family, and the isolation and sense of purpose really helped me focus and be thoughtful about the environment I was creating.

What advice do you have for adding bold design choices to a home, particularly for someone who might be intimidated by color or pattern?

My main advice would be not to overthink it. It's just a room, it's just a wall. You're not stuck with it if you hate it, so why not try something new? Change in all aspects of life is healthy and necessary, and that includes interior design. I love moving things around, trying different colors, different patterns. Good design should use what you enjoy as a foundation but push you just beyond your comfort zone. That's when your perspective is forced to shift a little, to grow, and the bold colors, textures, or ideas are no longer as intimidating.

Amid the color and pattern your home so masterfully embraces, white and negative spaces also play a dominant role. What do these visual breaks add to your home?

Negative space is important to avoid design becoming too cluttered or overwhelming. Your eyes need a place to rest and relax in order to appreciate the design elements. If there are too many things going on, you don't know where to look, and so you end up looking at and appreciating nothing. I do have a variety of patterns in the house, but there isn't a place where you can stand by one pattern and see the next. I did that on purpose—that pattern conflict would be too much on the senses and detract from the design elements of each separate space.

How have you created a home that is both design forward and family friendly for your three beautiful sons?

I consciously tried to design the house how I want it to look, but with realistic expectations. There are areas of the house, like the family room, that aren't my ideal in terms of design, but they are practical for a family of five. We all live in the house equally, but there are spaces that are just for the kids because it's important for them to be able to play and express themselves. We have a playroom in the basement, and the third floor is an open area where they can run around and play sports when the weather is bad. The walls up there are a bit banged up, but at the same time, the walls elsewhere don't get messed up since they have the freedom to do what they want in their spaces. And for anything in between, there's always the Magic Eraser!

You've designed your space with more than just your immediate family in mind; you also host large holiday gatherings.

I love to throw a party! Hosting family and friends is one of my favorite things to do, so it gives me great satisfaction when I'm able to do that in my own home. But it's more than just parties; it's so important to create and foster community. If you look into any research on happiness, invariably strong and vibrant communities are at the heart of the happiest cultures. For me, large gatherings of family and friends in my home are my favorite expression of community. Design choices can really add to those gatherings, but they don't require anything different or explicit. I want guests to feel as much at home in my house as my family does, so the same principles of creating appealing, relaxed, and inviting spaces apply. In fact, the better I design our home for my family, the better it will be for guests and large gatherings because it will feel comfortable, welcoming, and communal to them, too.

What is your most cherished item in your home?

The material contents of my house don't hold much sentimental value for me, with the exception of some of the things on my walls. I certainly appreciate and enjoy the things in my house, and they are all there for a reason, but the pieces on the walls are there because they each have made me feel something. I get genuine pleasure from looking at them. I still have some blank walls waiting to be filled because I would rather leave them empty than hang something I don't truly love and enjoy. I have multiple favorite pieces, which vary from pencil drawings done by my sister-in-law, to vintage art finds, to a large Alex Katz piece that hangs in the kitchen. I suppose, though, that if the house was burning down and everyone was outside, I would try to save the boys' art projects from over the years. Those are the only irreplaceable things.

How do you create or find moments of hygge in your home?

I think that what our family has been through with my son's illness and how we've coped with it has generated an inherent feeling of hygge between us and within the house. We spent so much time here together during my son's isolation period, and we really made the most of it. My husband and I don't discount the time we have with our children, and we go out of our way to make sure they feel safe and secure given all that has happened. Reading with them by the fire, doing art projects, playing sports, messing around outside— it's all normal stuff that takes on new meaning once it has been put at risk. Everyday togetherness is not something I take for granted.

"I have three favorite design elements: wallpaper, lighting, and art. Rooms are essentially empty boxes waiting to become something more interesting, and decorating the walls and ceilings really completes a space for me. People often focus on furniture as the primary components to a room, but the furniture can be secondary when your senses are drawn to the surrounding walls and art."

CHARM

We believe that interior design should be deeply personal. Spaces come to life in highly individual ways, reflecting the personalities, values, and priorities of the people who dwell within them. These homes showcase the unique point of view and inimitable style of each homeowner.

ANA GASTEYER

Actor | Comedian | Mother
BROOKLYN, NEW YORK

Christiana: We have always been huge *Saturday Night Live* fans. This may tell you a lot about how popular we were in high school, but many a Saturday night was spent at Aimee's house watching *SNL* (I swear we had friends). When a celebrity uses our wallpaper, we also get really excited—probably as a result of reading too many tabloid magazines in high school (we really did have friends!). So when Daniel Kanter of Manhattan Nest reached out to purchase wallpaper for a project he was working on with Ana Gasteyer, naturally, we freaked out. The project turned out beautifully, and we struck up a casual Instagram friendship with Ana. She was one of the first people who came to mind when we were deciding who to reach out to for this book, and to our surprise and delight, she agreed to be a part of it.

The thing that stood out to us the most when we met Ana was how incredibly down to earth she is and how beautifully her home captures and reflects her personality. Her house has a cozy eclecticism about it—furniture has been collected, handed down from relatives, and mixed with modern Ikea purchases. When we arrived, Ana was busy cleaning, joking about how she'd just returned from a work trip to find almost every kitchen cabinet door had been left open. We couldn't help but laugh at this seemingly universal frustration of living with people who don't share your own household priorities. But what we loved most about the home Ana has created was how obvious it was from the moment we stepped in the door that it was one centered around love, laughter, and family (even if the cabinets don't always find their way shut).

Your career takes you away from home for long stretches of time. Does that lifestyle make home even more special?

My home is definitely my haven; it's where I restore, connect, get grounded. The kitchen is the centerpiece of the apartment, big by New York City standards, and cooking is what I do to wind down. I like to cook in my kitchen, to entertain casually at the counter, and to putter around the rest of the place while something is on the stove. So I actively focus on restoring and maintaining order—putting things where they go, purging what we don't use. I do this because organized spaces make me feel calmer and because I know another gig is just around the corner, and I want to spend as little time as possible getting out the door. I'd rather spend my precious time talking to my children.

As for peace and calm, I worked with design blogger Daniel Kanter a few years ago to make my bedroom a haven. Long ago, I read this feng shui quote pointing out that, when it comes to decor, we so often focus on our public spaces and ignore our private ones. When our bedrooms are personal, cozy, and peaceful, we are essentially nurturing our quiet, private selves. This really resonated with me. I love my bedroom; it is my peaceful retreat. It's more beautiful than so many hotel rooms I stay in, and I am grateful every time I come home again.

You've used a few of our wallpapers throughout your home. What do you think these patterns bring to your space?

I think of wallpaper as a delightful surprise, a cool way to say, "Hey, check out this secret, joyful spot in your house that you forgot about." It's great in bathrooms because each time you pop in, it's a happy little reprieve from the world outside. I love the metallic sheen to the copper Andanza wallpaper behind our piano—our music area is one of my favorite things about our house. I've always felt that a piano turns a house into a home, and this wallpaper perfectly celebrates that idea. It is cozy, inviting, elegant, and fun, all at once. I rehearse and arrange music there for my act, my kids practice there, and we hire a piano player for parties—a great, old-fashioned move that instantly raises the party game. The space works in any of these situations.

What role do color and pattern play elsewhere in your home? How do you decide where and how to add these elements?

As I age, I find that I don't need an overload of pattern and color, but I'm essentially drawn to it. My home is a haven though, a retreat, so at this busy time in my life, I find that I prefer a predominantly blank canvas with life itself adding the color—children's art, a pretty bar, flowers. I think that's why I like wallpaper where I use it—it can be so effective in a small gesture, and encourage without overwhelming.

How do you create a home where family and loved ones can gather?

A family-friendly space is one that is open and available, with lots of surfaces for projects and soft places to settle. The goal in my apartment was to utilize the open, airy vibe to encourage gathering and connecting, while ensuring that the bedrooms were cozy and inviting retreats. I love the chalkboard for communicating. And I love that the central island, the dining table, and the coffee table all get utilized regularly, and that the bedrooms are safe havens. My bedroom was designed with the idea that kids and animals will inevitably pile in, so it can accommodate those sweet moments without imploding. Each kid has extra beds in their own rooms, as well as great mattresses, so that they feel safe and cozy at night.

How do you find or create hygge in your home?

Texture and color are, of course, key. I like the balance of sheepskins, velvet, and wood, along with plants and music. They bring in a sense of vitality and energy, and that means a lot to me. I also try to keep a balance between special relics—such as the mirror from my parents' home and the busts from my father-in-law—and useful, temporal furniture, like my Ikea sofa and dining table. Families need furniture that they don't have to stress out about to live in, laugh at, and celebrate on.

QUIRKY COLLECTIONS

Ana's work requires constant travel, and to commemorate her adventures, she collects creamers from each destination she visits. The hedgehog is her favorite, but each one functions as both an interesting everyday item that can be artfully displayed, as well as an atypical memento that reminds Ana of a specific project or experience.

GLENN LAWSON

Designer | Entrepreneur | Co-Owner of Lawson-Fenning

LOS ANGELES, CALIFORNIA

One of the best parts of our jobs has to be our frequent inspiration excursions. For quite some time, Lawson-Fenning has been a must-visit whenever we're in Los Angeles. It would not be an exaggeration to say that it's one of the best home decor boutiques in the country. Glenn Lawson and his business partner, Grant Fenning, have a remarkable ability to find unique, up-and-coming artists, and their eponymous collection of furniture and accents is the stuff of which interior design dreams are made. We reached out to Glenn on a whim and quickly struck up an email correspondence. Our conversations evolved into discussions about a wallpaper collaboration. Our Lawson-Fenning for Hygge & West collection was a joy to work on, and we're so thrilled that the patterns truly reflect the duo's unique Southern California aesthetic.

Glenn and his partner, Nima Dabestani, have created a special retreat on a hill overlooking Los Angeles, and we had a wonderful day with them while photographing their home. They're the kind of hosts who, when we noticed a cake in their fridge and joked about it looking good, immediately brought the cake out and insisted that we have some. It's always nice to meet individuals whose work you admire and find that they are also wonderful people, and Glenn is the perfect example of this.

Tell us about your home. How would you describe its style?

My home is a 1920s typical Spanish Revival. It was mostly original when I bought it, but had been painted bright red and yellow and had a bad 1970s bathroom and kitchen. Luckily, it still had the original layout, plaster, and fixtures. I had a lot of fun updating it, but I kept the original spirit and aesthetic in mind with every decision I made. I learned a lot about the proportion and detailing of Spanish houses during my research; there is a great unwritten rule with these houses that nothing matches. All of the windows are different sizes and the original hardware and lighting change from room to room. It makes it much easier to make design decisions because the variance allows for flexibility—each room can evolve into its own space. The house definitely dictates a lot. The bedrooms are downstairs and living spaces are up, with garden terraces on each level. It invites a sort of ritual between rest and work, or rest and play.

How often do you change the decor in your home?

I am constantly rotating in new pieces of furniture, art, and rugs. It never ends! Even rotating the same pieces into different rooms helps the house always feel fresh. I had a piece of art in the den for years. One day I decided to move it to another room and suddenly everyone who came over was remarking on it, even though they had seen it a million times before. I am fortunate to be able to rotate pieces in and out of the shop—it is a constant exchange. I think living with the pieces I sell makes the shop more authentic.

Your business and style have a seamless way of honoring the past while keeping an eye to the future. What is your advice for other homeowners who want to do the same?

I attach so much meaning to objects. Some of my favorite pieces aren't typically aesthetic choices. I think if you live with things you love, the space always works. I always have a nice balance of meaningful objects and inspiring art.

The color in your home appears in muted, grounded, earthy tones that complement, rather than compete with, the rest of the elements in your space. What inspired and informed your color palette?

I generally shy away from color. I like to think of the people who inhabit the space as the color. Most of the color I do have is pulled from the outdoors. I always advise people to paint a space a warm white. I'm not a big fan of color on walls—I save it for things that can be switched out, like art and textiles.

Some associate coziness with more—more objects, more textiles, more things. However, your home has an inherent warmth to it, while still maintaining clean lines and a sense of tasteful restraint. What, in your opinion, makes a home inviting, and how do you create coziness without clutter?

I live with a lot of objects, but I don't have everything out all at once. My mom was big on seasonal decoration. Every few months the house had a different feel based on the season or holiday. I do the same thing with objects, pillows, etc. I'm a big fan of the changing seasons and how it informs the choices you make at home. I move things around. I use them. There is nothing too precious.

Texture abounds in your home, from supple leather and plush velvet to earthy woven textiles and raw woods.

I use texture like other people use color. A whole space can be black and white (or warm matte black and cream, in my case), but if you have a variety of textures—rough and smooth, matte and gloss—the space really comes alive.

What is your most prized possession in your home?

For me, it's my dad's writing desk, which I now use as my bedside table. I was obsessed with it when I was growing up. The desk is early American and has great details, moving parts, and hidden drawers. It's like colonial origami. I grew up going to flea markets with my parents, which is how I learned about furniture like my dad's desk. That desk has so many great memories attached to it.

Joy—like design—is often in the details. What are the small pleasures or simple moments your home allows you to enjoy that bring you the most happiness?

One of my favorite things about the house is that it works well for when it's just the two of us, but it also has a perfect layout for entertaining. When I'm alone, it feels so quiet and contemplative. The light is incredible, and the garden is visible from every room. But my home really sings when it's full of family and friends. There are so many great spots to share a meal, watch movies, or just hang out.

SHELVES AS A MOOD BOARD

As a designer, Glenn is constantly looking for new ways to spark inspiration. The bookshelves in his study provide a spot to bring ideas to life in an unconventional way.

"Since I have a rotating array of objects, art, and pottery, I like to use my bookshelves as an opportunity to get inspired. I think of them as a three-dimensional mood board. I'm always putting little collections together. It helps me work out good color combinations, material combinations, and scale combinations. It also allows me to bring in new things and see how they mix. It helps me immensely in my design process to have a palette of colors and materials that I know work well together."

MALENE BARNETT

Artist | Mentor | Owner of Malene B.

BROOKLYN, NEW YORK

Christiana: The second of three first-generation American girls, born in the United States from Caribbean parentage, Malene Barnett has developed a playful island design aesthetic that is deeply rooted in her heritage. The second we pulled up to her stoop and spotted her bright-turquoise door, we knew her home was going to be special. Her vibrant smile and cheerful welcome was reflected in the warm yellow walls of her entry and in special touches throughout the home beyond.

Known first and foremost as the creator of the Malene B. design studio, Malene fell in love with carpet design while attending the Fashion Institute of Technology, and was able to launch her own brand of products after working in the industry for ten years. We connected with Malene several years ago over our mutual love of pattern and color, and we always look forward to seeing what beautiful new products she creates. As an example of her inspiration, after coming home from spending the day in her colorful yet serene home, it only took about a week for me to re-wallpaper my entry with a bright, pastel pink pattern—and it couldn't make me happier!

What inspires you in your work? In the design of your home?

I'm inspired by my Afro-Caribbean heritage, world travels, and handcrafted textiles. The inspiration behind my home is modern island living. I wanted my home to embrace island style while living in a city. My goal is to live in the Caribbean, but until then I want my space to feel as if I do already.

You've traveled to more than twenty-five countries. How has that travel influenced your design style?

Every time I travel, I learn about a culture, experience rituals, build relationships with the people, and immerse myself in the environment. I then use the experience as a source of inspiration to design. For example, my Wolof carpet design was inspired by my trip to Senegal, and my Mendhi design reinterprets the henna painting ceremony I experienced during my girlfriend's wedding in India.

Every culture has their own visual language that appears in their textiles and patterns. What can you learn about a country or culture just from their textiles?

You can learn so much! Textiles are like photographs—they document moments in time and everyday objects that we often take for granted. A culture's textiles and patterns tell stories of rituals, icons, and everyday life. The people who create them are storytellers, and every culture needs them to continue to celebrate their culture and keep their traditions alive.

Your home has beautiful moments of pattern, but it's not covered in pattern the way some might expect of a designer.

Even though I love pattern, I love space, too. I think patterns need space to breathe, and I do that by surrounding them with a complementary color. This allows the pattern to be highlighted, rather than lost, in the space.

Your home greets guests with a cheerful, bright-turquoise door—and it's the perfect preview of what they can expect once inside. Why was creating that first impression important to you and what message does it convey to visitors and passersby alike?

My home is a sacred space. I work, live, and spend a lot of time at home. The turquoise door influences the energy of anyone who passes through it, turning their focus to positivity before stepping inside. Visitors tell me they feel transported to a tranquil space and find it hard to leave. Passersby always stop in awe, smile, and take a picture. I think the door color inspires people to think differently about their own space.

What are your tips for working with color? What advice would you give someone who might be afraid to try something bold in their home?

Go for it! It's only paint. If you don't like it, you can just pick another color. If paint is too scary, then start by adding colorful textiles, decorative pillows, and art to your space. Start with a room you use often—your bedroom, for example. Then think about the mood you want to create. Do you want to wake up in a bright, airy room? If so, explore soft pastel shades, like lavender, yellows, and greens. Maybe you want a sultry sophisticated look. Then go bold with deep jewel tones, such as burgundy, navy, or even black. If you can't think of a mood, begin with your favorite color and explore its various shades, then decide how you would want to live with it. This was the approach I took in my own home. It's evident that turquoise is my favorite color, because it's plastered, in various shades, all over my house. I selected pastel shades of bold colors. When you select shades of strong colors, it tones down the color value. This creates a softer, more serene look and feel.

What do you love most about your home?

I love so many parts of my home, but I really love my floors. The teal-stained floors keep my home looking fresh and island-inspired. I also love the open floor plan on my parlor floor. The large glass windows in my kitchen provide a view of the backyard when sitting in the living room, which brings the outdoors inside. And I can't forget my bathroom—I'm lucky to have a spa-like bathroom for everyday use. I believe a home must have a unique style that is personal to the owner, plus rooms to rest, relax, dream, and create.

What's your most prized possession in this home?

The buffet in my living room; it was one of my mother's first pieces of furniture. The piece is modern, with classic, clean lines, simple silver hardware details, and a set of drawers and shelves for storage. Even at forty-four years old, it is still very much in style.

As a young child, the buffet was the centerpiece of our dining room. It evokes fond memories of my mother storing fine china and silverware that was passed down from her mother, my grandmother. She also made the top look pretty by displaying her crystal punch bowl and other decorative finds. I remember gathering around the dining room table for holiday dinners, when the buffet would become the serving station for all the food. When I have parties today, the buffet turns into the bar and I, too, use it to store my artwork and decorative pieces.

There's virtually nothing in your home that doesn't feel unique to you. What are your tips for adding yourself into your environment?

Think about what you truly love and continue to add it to your space. Your home is one of the few areas of your life that you can truly personalize, so just do it.

ANGELINA RENNELL

Designer | Artist | Owner of Beklina

LA SELVA BEACH, CALIFORNIA

We first met Angelina Rennell several years ago when she reached out to us with artwork for a possible wallpaper collaboration. She had heard about our company and felt a connection because she had a cat named Hygge. We loved her concepts, but at the time we were only producing screen-printed wallpaper—a technique that we knew couldn't capture the delicate watercolor feel of her art. Shortly after, our printer approached us with an opportunity: digitally printed, removable wallpaper tiles. We reached back out to Angelina and used her artwork to create our first, and to date only, removable wallpaper tiles collection. In the years since we'd launched our collaboration, Angelina has expanded her business, Beklina, to include a fashionable line of clothing and accessories, and a delightful, beautifully curated online shop of the same name. We've enjoyed seeing her business grow alongside ours and can't wait to see what comes next for her and her brand.

When we told Angelina about this book, she mentioned that her mother, Cynthia Williams, had an incredibly special and distinct beach home, called the Spaceship House, where she and her family spend weekends and holidays. The house was in desperate need of renovations when she and her mother first purchased it. Slowly, over a period of two years, the duo restored the home, embracing the quirks and challenges along the way and infusing their personal style throughout. It's clear upon visiting the house that this was a labor of love, and the end result is a truly one-of-a-kind home.

Tell us about the Spaceship House. What was your role in bringing it to life?

I lived in the most amazing homes growing up, and all of them have shaped me. I think of homes as our second body that we share with family. Home should be the happiest, safest, warmest, and most hygge place in our personal worlds. I discovered the Spaceship House three years ago—a magical moment for sure—and knew that my mother (who was looking for a new home) would go nuts over it, even though it was barely livable. Every wall, every window, almost every inch needed to be replaced or restored, and over the two years it took to bring it back to life, we worked together to decide what would be best for this house.

The yard and landscaping are very much incorporated into the overall feel and aesthetic of the house, from its modern, somewhat otherworldly design, to the way the interior often uses the outside as a focal point. Why was it important to bring the outdoors in?

It's a California thing. It's especially important for this small home to feel larger and more expansive, and that's accomplished by embracing the outdoor space. We have plants inside and out, keep the doors open, and are lucky to have lots of windows. The outside is always with us. We lose the boundary between what's outside and what's inside, especially when the weather is warm.

What was the biggest challenge in creating this home?

The Spaceship House has no closet space and no flat walls. Paring down to just the necessities was a challenge, and it continues to be one. It reminds me of travel, ironically, because you can only pack so much.

There's a great contrast in the home, between the white minimalism of the walls and furniture and some wonderful pops of bold textiles, prints, and patterns.

I'm very driven by color and textiles. I find places to bring them into my life, like the pillows and rugs. Pattern is visual rhythm and song. In a room, it adds texture, movement, emotion, and mood, and defines and unites objects within a space. I work from an emotional instinct, an almost subconscious level. Due to the Spaceship House's small size, it needs to remain open in order to feel large. Colors and prints actually enlarge the space instead of shrinking it; patterns invite the eye into another space or dimension.

We love that you named your cat Hygge! What is it about that word or concept that feels so special to you?

The moment that I read about the word *hygge* over a decade ago, I was instantly in love with it. I wrote it down on a note, and I knew I had to use that word and bring it into my life. What a wonderful, perfect concept. The word *cozy* is one of my favorites and expresses love, comfort, health, and nurturing; to me, hygge is that word in relation to home and lifestyle. And anyone who is a cat person knows that cats are the all-time embodiment of hygge, so I actually had the name before I even had the cat.

What is your most prized possession in your home?

My most prized possession is the leather kangaroo my mother bought before I was born. She walked into a showroom and bought the entire display: two leather couches, two orange velvet ottomans, and a leather kangaroo. I still have all the furniture pieces in my home, while the kangaroo lives here. Carmella, my oldest daughter, almost destroyed it when she was little, and a leather master had to coax it back to life. My mother convinced her that it was going to die if she didn't give it up.

What home design rule or guideline do you always follow?

I don't have any decorating or design rules, but the closest thing would be that my vision in all my spaces is to slowly, over a lifetime, get rid of things I don't like and replace them with ones I love. I deeply believe that I'm a happier person with more practical things that wear well over time and aren't fussy. In the last year I've learned to let go a little with messes and not to be too quick to make things perfect. There needs to be balance in how much you try to control a space, otherwise hygge will not be achieved.

COMMUNICATING THROUGH DESIGN

"The personal choices that most people wouldn't notice are what make this house a home—the objects that have been with us in every home, the reasons we made certain decisions, and how our ideas came to life. As much as I was involved in every single step of the process, the space is very much my mother. We have our own language and life-long conversation happening through style, arrangements, colors, and motifs."

STORM THARP

Artist | Plantsman | Cook
PORTLAND, OREGON

Aimee: I had the good fortune to work with Storm Tharp many years ago, when he was the creative director on one of my campaigns during my retail marketing days. I was completely taken by his warm, distinctive personality. Later, I learned that he was also an incredibly talented and successful artist and, captivated by his work, I closely followed his career over the years. When we decided to find homeowners in the Portland area to feature in this book, I knew Storm would be a great addition, and I couldn't wait to reconnect with him.

Storm and his partner, Mike Blasberg, have created a thoroughly charming, welcoming home in a handsome neighborhood of Portland. Their love of art and music is evident throughout, as are their adept green thumbs. Almost everything in the home has a story of the person or event that connected the couple with the item, and we loved learning more about Storm and Mike's lives, friends, and interests. At the end of the day, we sat together in the front yard, sipping on Mike's delicious gin and tonics, and visiting like old friends, even though most of us had only just met that day. We hope to return sometime soon to hear more stories and sample some of the cooking for which Storm is known.

What was it like growing up in the small rural town of Ontario, Oregon? How, if at all, did that influence your home today?

There used to be an idea of Main Street that epitomized a Western town. I think of *The Last Picture Show*, for example, as a place that is both tough and naïve at the same time. This may not make sense to many modern people, but for me, it represented a kind of optimism that really defined how the western states exemplified America. It was so much about small business and family, and supplying just enough for a community. It was never about the rest of the world. It was always about the necessity of what was immediately possible. It's a simple kind of thinking that I really admire and miss. People did the best with what they had, and frankly, that was a lot. My mom's family distributed beer and wine. My Aunt Pat had a ladies' clothing boutique called The Vogue. My Grandma Lou flew a plane! Incredible stuff. But that world has changed, and in some ways, that potential has vanished. Main Street is often vacant, and it's sad to me. In Eastern Oregon, you have a large, dignified Japanese community, a vital Hispanic community, and one of the few, thriving Basque communities in America. This creates a dynamic narrative that I rarely encounter anywhere anytime, anymore. So how has that influenced my home? Well, the cowboy, the farmer, the Japanese, and the Basque are evident throughout our home. I am such a product of that culture. My first Navajo blanket was a gift from my Basque grandpa. It's everywhere in my life now.

How would you describe the style of your home? Is it similar to that of your art?

Most people I know recognize the way I live in the work I make. There is a graphic quality and a nostalgia in certain things that is hard for me to shed. I realize that those two qualities have almost nothing in common; however, in this regard, they come together by way of a movie poster, or a record cover, or a book. These vessels represent dreams as much as they represent a timeline of their own craft and the method of their existence. So much of how our home is portrayed has everything to do with something that has come before it, something we like. And in this way, my artwork is also a product of its interests. My work is full of footnotes, and I share them openly. Our home is idiosyncratic, earthy, and colorful as much as it is spare, sculptural, and collected. I rarely live with anything that I don't love. If it's not special, I can't see it.

The focus and medium for your work is ever evolving and constantly shifting. Do you feel that same need for change and evolution in your home?

Yes, but I have gotten to that age where I am interested in the timeless. So regardless of the fact that I love ikat prints or South American textiles, I use them sparingly. That said, there is a part of me that will always address those affinities and showcase that appreciation in some way. My home decorating has never been embarrassing or subject to trends the way my wardrobe has, for example. I think back on the high and low interiors of my past, and I love all of them. I have always embraced bold color, graphic prints, and a mix of the rare and everyday.

What tips do you have for others who want to add art to their walls but are intimidated by the process?

I cannot state vehemently enough how gratifying it feels to bring artwork into your home. For one, you are helping sustain the creative life, which feels increasingly impossible and exceedingly essential. Secondly, these objects join you. They hook into you. You make them live, and in turn, they enrich your life. This is a fact. Like the walls of your home, they breathe life. Acquiring art is profoundly enriching. What art collecting should never be is tasteful. Please! Of course, an object may reflect an affinity you have with color or form, but the main purpose is that it inspires you and, even if it's hideous or violent, I believe it should comfort you as if you've always known it. The art on your walls should be bold and adventurous. I cannot stand tasteful art, and I abhor it as a decorative tool or status symbol. Your art should flirt with the reckless; if it's too nice, it's probably not good enough. Your art should be held to the same standards you have in people: exceptional, interesting, and crush-worthy.

In addition to your career as an artist, you're also a passionate cook.

Cooking for me is the most useful creative tool, which may sound surprising coming from an artist. Making art is mercurial and emotionally challenging. Bringing a delicious meal to the table after a tough day in the studio helps me feel like I've actually accomplished something. Preparing dinner for Mike or a small group of friends helps me maintain the ideals of sharing, hospitality, and creativity.

You have so many wonderful displays of objects throughout your space. Why is it important to you to be able to see these items?

Seeing affinities and recognizing preferences is just something I have always been drawn to and engaged with in some way. I think it's how I figured out who I was. An object on the shelf is hardly different from music on the turntable—it's a reflection. I enjoy the idea that all of those still lifes around the house are like sentences in some beautiful poem. Nothing on view is random or neglected. The objects in our home are actively narrative. I am acutely conscious of all of them.

If you had to select one item from your home to represent who you are, what would it be?

The dining room table (on page 221). It's an English farm table made of pine that I inherited after my parents got divorced. It has great bones and some awesome scars. I believe it fell off the back of a truck and skidded facedown across the pavement when my parents were moving from one home to another. But it's not just nostalgia that has me hooked. I really appreciate the proportions. It was never intended to be a dining table—my parents used it as a sofa table. It's narrow and hard to sit a bunch of people around, which makes it wonderful. Our dinner parties are always crowded and loud and intimate. It feels just right to me.

There's a sense of fun, playfulness, and not taking yourself too seriously in your home. How is that a reflection of who you are and how you live in your home?

I'm not sure if it's a reflection of who we are as much as it's a reflection of what we can afford. I don't mean to sound cavalier. We are very fortunate, but as you can see, many items in our home we have either made or found. I still use milk crates to prop up plants. The living room is almost entirely secondhand, except for the rugs. When you find yourself collecting in this way, you stop taking it all so seriously. On some level, you buy it because it's affordable and maybe not even valuable, and therefore not precious. Then, twenty-five years later, you realize you have some really lovely things. It's inherently easygoing.

TREATING PLANTS AS ART

"The plants are the greatest feature of our home. I love them like family, talk to them, and nurture them. We even name them. I have said many times that I feel the plants are my true artwork. The plants have big personalities, and they grow and change before our eyes. Their nature is not static— it's conversational. If you removed the plants from our home, you would remove the lightness and the sense of humor. Our plants change the chemistry of the room."

LIZ KAMARUL

We sparked up an Instagram friendship with Liz Kamarul, a highly regarded stylist and design consultant, after being introduced to her through an old friend from high school. We were irresistibly drawn to her unique style and free-spirited design aesthetic, so it came as no surprise when we learned that she'd moved into a 1982 Winnebago with her husband, Tim, and their two adorable dogs, Cudi and Bo. After realizing they both wanted to make a big change in the direction of their lives, they decided to quit their jobs, rent out their house, and hit the open road.

We caught up with Liz and Tim on the coast near Santa Cruz, California, and were so inspired not only by the way they'd created such a special, personality-filled home-on-the-move, but also by how seamlessly they'd transitioned into their vagabond lifestyle. It made us realize that it really is never too late—or too early—to make big changes and pursue the life you desire. Their cozy camper also goes to show that you can create a happy home no matter its shape or size.

What made you decide to purchase the RV?

We wanted a simpler life, full of adventure, and the idea of living in an RV with few items and no itinerary while exploring the country was a dream come true. We were tired of the routine life we were living and wanted to walk away from that; we felt that breaking down and rebuilding would be a great life-changing experience.

The motto of our trip is, "What do I desire?" which is a quote from the philosopher Alan Watts. We were really inspired by one of his talks about how people spend their lives working so they can continue living the lives they're unhappy with, which is to continue working, resulting in an unhappy cycle. We realized that life was so much more, and we desired experiences and time together. We've all been raised to believe that life has to look a certain way, and we wanted to break that mold.

What inspired your Winnebago design and what was the creation process like?

The Winnebago is bohemian-inspired, like our home was, but it's a neutral version with fewer items. We knew we wanted to have all white walls to keep it as bright as possible, so we leaned toward a Scandinavian aesthetic. The design process itself was fairly similar to the process for our home and was done only on the weekends for about five months before we left on our adventure. I didn't spend a lot of time agonizing over decisions—when I found a product that I liked, I just went with it. I think the most impactful part of our design is the wallpaper, most of which Tim and I put up together. The most difficult part was probably the carpet in the cab—a process that required Tim to cut hundreds of small pieces of carpet to mold around the different areas on the cab floor.

You've used a lot of pattern in the Winnebago—including our Wood wallpaper by Askov Finlayson. What does pattern bring to a small space?

Because we can't have a lot of physical items in the RV, bringing in the wallpaper helped add character to the space without clutter. I think it made the Winnebago come to life.

How did your dogs, Cudi and Bo, influence the way you designed your RV?

The biggest challenge with the dogs was finding a place for them to sit while we drive. We added some hooks under the dining area so we could attach them with their harnesses on short leashes, and then we set a bed down for them to comfortably ride in.

How has life in a Winnebago enabled you to connect with nature?

Living in the Winnebago has allowed us to live in a different landscape every day: on the beach, in the woods, or in the city. We definitely spend more time outside now, especially during meals. It's great to be able to sit and look at the ocean one day and be immersed in the woods the next. I think being somewhere new each day is helping us avoid routine, which is exactly what we wanted to accomplish on this trip. We never know if we're going to be relaxing on the beach or hiking a trail, and not knowing is part of the fun. It's all about being open to experience and willing to go with the flow.

RESOURCES

AESOP

Aesop makes the most amazing hand wash of all time, hands down. Is it a splurge? Yes. But the scent makes it worth every penny.

www.aesop.com

ANIMAL PRINT SHOP

Sharon Montrose's adorable, artful images work in nearly any setting. We've used them in our own homes, and they are also featured in several of the homes in this book.

www.theanimalprintshop.com

ASKOV FINLAYSON

We were in love with this menswear brand and boutique long before we collaborated with them on a wallpaper collection. The Marvel Bar–inspired candles are divine, and we both proudly wear our North hats all winter long.

204 N First Street
Minneapolis, MN 55401
www.askovfinlayson.com

BEKLINA

This online boutique showcases owner Angelina Rennell's (featured on page 212) keen eye for design in apparel and home goods as well as her eponymous line of clothing.

www.beklina.com

BLU DOT

This Minneapolis-based furniture company creates well-made, modern designs. Their work can be spotted not only in both of our own homes, but also in many of the homes throughout this book.

www.bludot.com

CANOE

Our favorite stop while we were shooting in Portland, this shop is truly a design lover's dream. They feature an impeccably curated assortment of home goods, accessories, and jewelry, and the owner is simply delightful.

1233 SW 10th Avenue
Portland, OR 97205
www.canoe.design

CHESTER WALLACE

Owned by Patrick Long and Jon Hart (featured on page 52), Chester Wallace bags are as utilitarian as they are attractive. They are all handmade in Portland and are fantastic for both work and travel.

www.chesterwallace.com

CORAL & TUSK

With a wide array of beautifully embroidered patterns, Stephanie Housley's (featured on page 32) company is one of our favorite sources for throw pillows, table linens, and gifts.

www.coralandtusk.com

DEKOR

Isabelle Dahlin's (featured on page 62) eclectic aesthetic carries through into the assortment of home goods and accessories featured in her shop, with locations in Los Angeles and Ojai.

3191 Glendale Boulevard
Los Angeles, CA 90039
105 S Montgomery Street
Ojai, CA 90039
www.dekorla.com

EDEN & EDEN

A personal favorite of ours, Eden & Eden is the perfect little boutique. Owner (and good friend) Rachel Eden has curated an interesting mix of vintage and new home goods, clothes, and accessories. We are especially big fans of her jewelry selection.

560 Jackson Street
San Francisco, CA 94133
www.edenandeden.com

FARIBAULT WOOLEN MILL

Based in Faribault, Minnesota, the Faribault Woolen Mill has been in operation for almost 150 years. Their iconic collection of wool blankets and throws manages to make even Minnesota winters feel warm and cozy.

1500 NW 2nd Avenue
Faribault, MN 55021
www.faribaultmill.com

FERM LIVING

We are longtime admirers of this distinctive line of Danish contemporary designs—including furniture, home accessories, throw pillows and more—all with a touch of midcentury charm.

www.fermliving.com

FORNASETTI

What can we say? We're addicted. Our favorite way to celebrate business and life milestones is with these gorgeous, often cheeky plates. We find that Farfetch has the best selection and the best prices for Fornasetti products.

www.fornasetti.com
www.farfetch.com

FRAMEBRIDGE

To say that Framebridge has been a game-changer would be an understatement. They offer incredibly high-quality framing (and photo printing) at unbelievably low prices.

www.framebridge.com

HAPTIC LAB

Haptic Lab's quilts, featuring stitched city maps or constellations, are a wonderful way to bring color, texture, and a sense of place into your home decor.

www.hapticlab.com

HEATH CERAMICS

One of the most respected names in American design, Heath Ceramics' tiles, dinnerware, and home accessories elevate any occasion or corner of your home. Collaborating with them on a wallpaper collection was definitely a bucket list item for both of us.

www.heathceramics.com

JAYSON HOME

We've loved this shop since our days living in Chicago, and it's been so fun to see them grow and evolve over the years. This is one of our go-to resources for furniture and accessories, and they also have a beautiful selection of books.

1885 N Clybourn Avenue
Chicago, IL 60614
www.jaysonhome.com

LAWSON-FENNING

For us, no trip to Los Angeles would be complete without a visit to one of Lawson-Fenning's two locations (or both!). Featuring a truly stunning collection of home decor, art, and their own line of meticulously crafted furniture, there is not a single item in their assortment that we wouldn't love to own. Glenn Lawson is featured on page 192.

6824 Melrose Avenue
Los Angeles, CA 90038
1618 Silver Lake Blvd.
Los Angeles, CA 90027
www.lawsonfenning.com

LOWELL

We always love browsing the unique selection of pottery, jewelry, and home accessories found at Lowell. With a quirky, considered blend of vintage and new pieces, the shop feels more like a gallery than a store.

819 N Russell Street
Portland, OR 97227
www.lowellportland.com

MALENE B. STUDIO

With something for every surface of your home, Malene B. Studio offers rugs, tiles, and wallpapers with a colorful, global point of view designed by Malene Barnett (featured on page 202).

362 Halsey St, Studio One
Brooklyn, NY 11216
www.maleneb.com

MCAD ART SALE

While this only takes place in Minneapolis, Minnesota, it's so good that people travel from all over the country to attend. Minneapolis College of Art and Design is one of the nation's best design schools and this sale, occurring every November, features thousands of pieces by students and recent graduates. We never miss it.

www.mcad.edu/about-mcad/events
/art-sale

MQUAN STUDIO

Michele Quan's handmade ceramic art and objects for the home and garden are truly stunning in their simplicity. We love the meanings behind the symbols that adorn each piece.

www.mquan-studio.myshopify.com/

PAPER JAM PRESS

These graphic, hand-printed letterpress posters always make us smile. They're a must for any old-school hip-hop fan.

www.paperjampress.com

THE PERISH TRUST

This modern day general store, co-owned by Rod Hipskind (featured on page 120), mixes unique, local handiwork with carefully selected vintage pieces and is a must-visit when in San Francisco.

728 Divisadero Street
San Francisco, CA 94117
www.theperishtrust.com

REFLECTIONS COPENHAGEN

We discovered this company in Copenhagen, which features a stunning collection of crystal mirrors and candleholders, and instantly fell madly in love.

www.reflections-copenhagen.com

ROOM & BOARD

This Minnesota-based company is committed to producing high-quality, well-designed furniture right here in the United States. Their simple, clean designs work with any home aesthetic, and their customer service is without equal.

www.roomandboard.com

SAFFRON MARIGOLD

An excellent source for fair-trade, hand block-printed table linens. We're both devotees of their table cloths and napkins and love the quality of the fabric as well as the bold patterns and colors.

www.saffronmarigold.com

SCHOOLHOUSE ELECTRIC

Schoolhouse Electric is our go-to shop for beautiful lighting and home accessories, and we love their selection hardware. It's always our first stop for finding exactly what we're looking for.

2181 NW Nicolai Street
Portland, OR 97210
27 Vestry Street
New York, NY 10013
www.schoolhouse.com

SF RUGS

A go-to website for one-of-a-kind vintage rugs. We love their curated selection, sourced during the owner's travels.

www.sfrugs.com

SKANDINAVISK

We met one of the owners, Shaun, during our time in Copenhagen and loved learning about his connection to the concept of hygge and the stories behind all of their Scandinavian-inspired scents.

www.skandinavisk.com

TAMAR MOGENDORFF

These handmade objects and decorations are one-of-a-kind and add an endearing, eye-catching touch to any space for any age.

www.tamarmogendorff.com

TINA FREY

Tina Frey's modern resin pieces are an absolute favorite of ours, both for our personal homes as well as gifts for loved ones. We're especially taken by her playful Lapin collection.

1278 Minnesota Street
San Francisco, CA 94106
www.tinafreydesigns.com

WORKSHOP

During our stay in Jackson Hole, Wyoming, we visited this warm, lovely shop. Workshop carries a fun collection of locally made jewelry and gifts and also has a large assortment of Coral & Tusk products, made by Stephanie Housley (featured on page 32). Stop at Persephone Bakery for some treats, then head over to this boutique for a treat of a different kind.

180 East Deloney Avenue
Jackson, WY 83001
www.workshopjh.com

ACKNOWLEDGMENTS

Many thanks to Deanne, Vanessa, and the Chronicle team for shaping our words, photos, and ideas into a truly beautiful book. Melissa, your thoughtful contributions were essential to this project—we could not have done this book without you. James, we thank you for all your hard work and dedication in creating such exquisite images. We know it wasn't an easy time, which is why huge thanks are also in order for Nils for his assistance and positive energy. Murray, thank you for taking us under your wing ten years ago and being patient with our many questions and mistakes. We love you and everyone at Artisan. Jason and Kathy, you always go above and beyond, and we are so grateful.

Aimee: Quite simply, I owe everything to the love and support of my friends and family. Christiana, there is no way to properly thank you for everything over our many years of friendship. You can be my wingman anytime. I somehow lucked out and have the three best boys in the world. Manny, thank you for the extraordinary life you've given me. MJ and Jackson, being your mom is my favorite job. I don't have a lot of friends, but the ones I have mean the world to me. You know who you are, and you know that I love you. Corey, you inspire me with your strength and your kindness. Love you, little sister. My mother, Faye, always made everything beautiful, from our house to all our family events. I love you, Mom—thank you for everything. And yes, we can buy flowers for the table. My father, Jerry, passed away while we were writing this book. Dad, you taught me to be a strong person, a successful business owner and a devoted spouse and parent with your exceptional example. I love you and miss you.

Christiana: I will forever be indebted to my wonderful friends for their kindness, encouragement, and support during my H&W adventure. There are not enough thank-yous, so I will just have to buy you more cocktails. Aimee, you are, as they say, the best of the best, and I'm beyond grateful for you and our lifelong friendship. Sarah and Bob, thank you for welcoming me into your East Bay livin' even when I don't help with the gardening. My love and gratitude to Joe. Not a day goes by that I don't feel lucky to have met you. To Jonathan, Beth, Eli, and David, thank you for making me part of your home and always making me laugh. I love you guys. And for my mom and dad, Kenneth and Angela, your unconditional love and support has been the greatest influence in my life. The way you live your own lives and the love you have for each other and our family has been an endless inspiration to me. I know exactly what home means because of you. I love you and thank you with all my heart.